U.S. Policy and the Two Koreas

Edward A. Olsen

**World Affairs Council
of Northern California
San Francisco, California**

**Westview Press
Boulder, Colorado
London, U.K.**

U.S. POLICY AND THE TWO KOREAS

Published in 1988 in the United States of America by the World Affairs Council of Northern California, 312 Sutter Street, Suite 200, San Francisco, California 94108

Distributed by Westview Press, Inc., 5500 Central Avenue, Boulder, Colorado 80301

Library of Congress Cataloging-in-Publication Data

Olsen, Edward A.

    U.S. policy and the two Koreas/by Edward A. Olsen.
      p.   .cm.
    Bibliography: p.
    ISBN 0-8133-0593-4
    1. United States—Foreign relations—Korea. 2. Korea—Foreign relations—United States. I. Title: US policy and the two Koreas.
E183.8.K6044 1987
327.730519—dc19   87-30045
                                                CIP

Printed and bound in the United States of America
by Linzee International Corporation

6   5   4   3   2   1

To my wife, Soon-hong,
who continually helps
my understanding of Korea.

CONTENTS

FOREWORD

This study is the culmination of a project on "U.S. Policy and the Two Koreas" conducted by the World Affairs Council of Northern California and funded by the John D. and Catherine T. MacArthur Foundation.

The Council's aim was to examine policy in a part of the world that has long been on our list of national concerns, but which has not received sufficient attention in recent years. As it happened, the political transition in South Korea and the American public's growing awareness that Korea has become an economic force to be reckoned with has brought renewed interest in the Korean peninsula in recent months.

The World Affairs Council project was built around the work of its director, Dr. Edward A. Olsen, Professor of National Security Affairs at the Naval Postgraduate School in Monterey, California. A study group comprised of men and women with strong and professional concerns with Korean and East Asian affairs met with Dr. Olsen nine times in 1987 to examine various facets of the U.S.-Korea nexus. We were joined at these sessions, and at a final conference on January 9, 1988, by American and Korean diplomats, scholars, and business leaders.

On behalf of the Study Group members, I should like to say that we are pleased that this fine work appears at a time when not only America's but the world's attention is increasingly focused on Korean affairs. We hope that Dr. Olsen's analysis and suggestions for amendments to American practice and policy will stimulate long overdue debate.

The views in this work are, of course, Dr. Olsen's alone. They do not express the views of the Study Group, the World Affairs Council, the MacArthur Foundation, the Naval Postgraduate

School, or the U.S. Government. I stress this point so that readers, especially Koreans on both sides of the 38th parallel, do not get the impression that this study is, in any sense, semiofficial.

We do hope that the project will contribute ideas and energy to a fresh look at Korean-American relations, on both sides of the Pacific.

Eugene B. Mihaly
Chairman

EXECUTIVE SUMMARY

South Korea and North Korea have come a long way since their devastation in the Korean War. South Korea today is a strong U.S. ally, possesses a dynamic economy, and is a regionally important state. North Korea, too, has made considerable economic and military progress.

Though the U.S.-South Korea relationship is essentially sound, and very important to the United States' other Northeast Asian ally (Japan), significant problems exist. The U.S. is experiencing economic difficulties and is overextended strategically at a time of rapid South Korean economic growth. This raises the questions of how bilateral economic relations might be improved, and whether it would be wise to have South Korea relieve the U.S. of some military burdens. Furthermore, U.S. policy toward Korea is faced with significant changes in Korean politics and inter-Korean relations. Consequently, it is important that Americans pay more attention to Korea.

This study examines these and related issues in the light of South Korea's economic and military maturation. It urges continued U.S. support for a valued Korean ally and trade partner. However, it recommends a major restructuring of the ways in which the U.S. keeps its commitments to South Korea. It calls for a new priority within U.S. interests, placing economics first. The following are the key recommendations, offered in accord with the suggested new priorities.

Economic Recommendations. The United States should:
• stress that economic strength is a crucial determinant of national power which increasingly shapes U.S. security and political relations with allies such as South Korea and adversaries such as North Korea;

• confront candidly the political imperatives of U.S. economic nationalism and frustration as Americans cope with Asian trade challenges;

• devise an overall U.S. policy toward the East Asian trade challenge, focusing primarily on Japan, that can legitimately be applied to South Korea;

• increase U.S. political pressures on Seoul to obtain desirable economic concessions;

• expand American lobbying efforts in South Korea to support U.S. economic goals;

• increase American understanding of how South Korean economic policy is made, so that Americans can more effectively influence those decisionmaking processes;

• strengthen the interdependent bonds between U.S. and South Korean economic and defense ties which make the alliance increasingly important;

• stress in a positive manner the *sophisticated* trade-defense linkages that could become powerful influence for the U.S. Government and private sector in American economic relations with South Korea;

Strategic Recommendations. The United States should:

• keep American forces in Korea but in an altered configuration, in which U.S. components would play a more flexible, dual-functioned regional role, and Republic of Korea (R.O.K.) forces would defend South Korea in a more self-reliant manner;

• establish an explicit timetable for shifting security burdens within the U.S.-R.O.K. alliance to make it more compatible with U.S. global priorities in an era of fiscal and strategic constraints and R.O.K. burgeoning economic capabilities;

• seek increased regional strategic cooperation of the U.S., R.O.K., and Japan by diminishing the United States' role between its Northeast Asian allies, while urging Japan and South Korea to pursue an expansion of political, economic, *and* military cooperation in their own national interests;

• restructure the Combined Forces Command into a more efficient organization so that South Koreans command Korean forces charged with South Korea's defenses, and Americans command forces in

Korea simultaneously tasked with Korean and flexible regional security;

• strengthen conventional defense in Korea to foster R.O.K. self-reliance and raise the nuclear threshold on the Korean peninsula; *Political Recommendations.* The United States should:

• encourage democratic pluralism, and be more assertive in opposing further military intervention;

• be realistic about the levels and variants of democracy likely to develop in South Korea; do not expect U.S.-style democracy; *Regional Recommendations.* The United States should:

• back bilateral Korean, and multilateral, efforts to reduce Korean tensions through negotiations;

• learn more about North Korea—the Democratic People's Republic of Korea (D.P.R.K.)—to prepare itself for eventual formal relations;

• be prepared to take advantage of future opportunities for such relations;

• emulate South Korea's flexibility toward the U.S.S.R. and P.R.C. by adopting comparable flexibility toward North Korea;

• not oppose sound proposals for the eventual unification of Korea and appreciate any increment of reduced tension such proposals may yield;

• seek reduced U.S.-D.P.R.K. tensions through expanded trade, cultural, scholarly, and scientific exchanges; and

• try to influence Pyongyang, and do not forfeit North Korea to perpetual Soviet influence.

PREFACE

The United States has been deeply involved in Korean affairs for more than forty years. August 1988 will mark the fortieth anniversary of the birth of the Republic of Korea which Americans helped establish. Thousands of Americans fought and died in Korea. Many more thousands of Americans have served in South Korea as part of a military deterrence system, as diplomats, as aid officials, or in private capacities. They have helped to keep South Korea safe from a North Korean renewal of the war stalemated more than thirty years ago and to achieve prosperity. In the decades since the Korean War truce was signed, the U.S. has played crucial governmental and commercial roles in assisting South Korean economic development. Despite this protracted involvement, many Americans—until relatively recently—did not pay much attention to Korea.

Americans need to pay more attention to Korean affairs for a variety of reasons. South Korea is one of the most dynamic states in the Pacific Basin, a region of rising importance to the U.S. and U.S.S.R. This is especially important in economic terms. This change in world affairs is occurring simultaneously with, and is a partial cause of, a diminished ability by the U.S. to assure the continuation of "Pax Americana." U.S. power and influence is declining relative to the growing stature of many of our trade partners and allies. This broad trend applies to U.S.-South Korean relations. It also has profound implications for U.S.-North Korean relations.

Three contemporary events piqued renewed American interest in Korea. The growth of the South Korean economy made it a factor in the collective East Asian trade challenge to U.S. interests. Though led and dominated by Japan, several other countries loom large in that challenge—the R.O.K. prominent among them. Seoul's widely publicized political instability in 1987, in the wake of seemingly comparable Philippine instability in 1986–87, caught the U.S. public's attention. Lastly, the prospect of the 1988 Seoul Olympics—in one of the world's geopolitical hot spots—focused global attention on Korea. Because of these events, and others discussed in the following analysis, Korea has assumed heightened visibility on the United States' horizon. The importance of U.S. policy toward Korea assumes an added dimension in 1988 because it is a U.S. presidential election year when Americans shall select someone who must cope with changes in U.S.-Asian relations, including significant developments in U.S.-Korean affairs.

The purpose of this study is to assess the efficacy of U.S. policy toward Korea and suggest ways in which some troubled portions of it might be improved. Despite the upbeat aspects of U.S.-South Korea relations, there are significant problems. U.S.-North Korea relations are marked by still more severe problems. All of these problems need to be addressed in the broad context of the United States' relations with a dynamic Pacific Basin.

This study is aimed at an audience with substantial background in world, Asian, and—to a lesser extent—Korean affairs. It does not deal minutely with the evolutionary details of contemporary U.S.-Korean relations or their international setting. However, for the general reader, and so that specialists understand the author's perceptions of the Korean frame of reference, substantial sections on the evolution of Korean affairs are included. These focus on postwar U.S.-Korean relations, key contemporary issues in security, economic, and political relations, and important factors in Korea's international setting. These sections offer relatively orthodox interpretations.

The main portion of the monograph consists of recommendations for improving U.S. policy toward Korea. Alternative policies and priorities are suggested. They do not fit wholly within either a liberal or a conservative agenda, but contain elements of both. They are non-partisan; appropriate for virtually any U.S. administration. A theme common to all the recommendations is pursuit of U.S. national interests within the context of more equitable collective security and economic interdependence in the international system. Consequently, they treat U.S.-Korean relations in a broad framework. Together, the proposals constitute a restructured blueprint for conducting U.S. relations with the two Koreas. However, it is not the only alternative "blueprint" available. Americans face a mosaic of choices.

The proposals are intentionally provocative, hoping to expand the range of (what many observers assume to be) realistic policy options. The recommendations are pointedly designed to stimulate a much needed reassessment in the U.S. about the wisdom of existing policy and the feasibility of alternative policies. I hope this study will provoke a long-overdue debate among Americans and Koreans about what is, and is not, sound in U.S. policy toward Korea.

1 The Evolution of U.S.-Korean Relations: 1945 to the 1980s

The transformation of U.S.-Korean relations between 1945 and the 1980s is an amazing phenomenon. When Americans entered Korea in the fall of 1945, after defeating the Japanese Empire, they found themselves in a backwater of world affairs. Korea's place in the overall scheme of U.S. foreign policy was minor. In the ensuing decades Korea evolved in numerous ways into a much more important place.

Though few of the Americans entering Korea in 1945 realized it, their presence was a return engagement and not the start of something new. The U.S. first became involved in Korean affairs in the 1870s, and first established diplomatic relations with a Korean state in 1882. In 1982 there was a considerable stir in the small circle of people actively concerned with U.S.-Korean affairs, and a centennial of sorts was celebrated. Though most Americans and South Koreans involved in that celebration were aware of the ironies of celebrating a full hundred-year cycle, it was left to the North Koreans to boldly point out that the "emperor's new clothes"—while not non-existent—were clearly threadbare in spots. Their pique stemmed from commemorating an imperialist treaty (albeit relatively benign) that eventually led to American acquiescence in Japan's oppressive colonization of Korea.

This commemoration rankled the nationalist consciousness of many South Koreans. They did not enjoy flaunting a hundred-year relationship that, from the late nineteenth century through the Yalta and Potsdam conferences, encompassed what many Koreans perceived to be American callousness regarding Korea. The centennial celebration symbolized the ambiguity felt by many South Koreans about their relationships with the U.S. today. Although most South Koreans understand the importance of U.S.-R.O.K.

relations to their country, the necessity of depending upon Americans rankles Korean sensitivities because of these facets of our history. Only joint action by South Koreans and Americans, who wanted to stress the durability and depth of contemporary U.S.-R.O.K. relations, validated the "centennial" celebration. Actually, the event stemmed from the relationship that has grown and flourished between the U.S. and southern Korea since 1945. That many Americans overlooked earlier flaws, were insensitive to Korean feelings of ambiguity, and ignored the other half of the Korean nation was barely tolerable for South Korean intellectuals and leaders during the 1982 centennial. However, it was accepted with some relish because it was useful for Seoul in cementing ties with the then new Reagan administration that had been damaged in earlier administrations, and it so visibly upset their North Korean adversaries.

The adversarial relationship between the two halves of Korea is *the* key reality of modern Korean affairs. In chicken-and-egg fashion it is simultaneously the cause and effect of the love/hate relationship embodied in much of contemporary U.S.-R.O.K. ties. Many Koreans justifiably blame the two major powers that emerged from World War II—the U.S. and the U.S.S.R.—for Korea's division. Had it not been for major power tension over the shape of the postwar peace, Korea might not have been divided. Neither would either modern Korean state be a protege of the postwar superpowers, nor would all the problems between the Koreas have surfaced. Internal repression by each security conscious state would have been less easy to justify. Consequently, while many South Koreans are grateful for all that the U.S. has done to keep their country alive and well, they also know that few of those dilemmas would have occurred had the U.S. not contributed to Korea's division. This, too, feeds Korean ambiguity.

Korea became a localized focus of Cold War tensions; one of the few that ultimately was transformed into a hot war. U.S. entry into new nationbuilding and geopolitical roles in Korea was poorly considered. Unlike the Soviet Union, which harbored longstanding ambitions vis-a-vis Asia it hoped to implement in the postwar era, U.S. planning for postwar East Asia focused on dismantling

2

the Japanese empire and helping those domains return to some semblance of normality. From Washington's perspective, Korea was only one of several byproducts of defeating Japan, and not a particularly important one.

Postwar U.S. policy in Asia focused on Japan and China. The U.S. effort in China emphasized helping an ally recover from a costly war. China's civil war and the victory of the communists was traumatic for the U.S., causing a rancorous and lengthy fissure in the United States' Asia policy. China quickly became a major adversary. In contrast, vanquished Japan just as quickly became the new fulcrum of U.S. policy in Asia. Because of its potential, which was speedily realized, Japan became the center of superpower attentions. The U.S. made its interests in Japan the cornerstone of its postwar Asia policy. Though China has again come to the fore since the Nixon overtures for U.S.-P.R.C. normalization, Japan properly remains the cornerstone of U.S. policy as it has been since the late 1940s.

The U.S. had no clear interests in Korea circa 1945. Only as Washington was able to define its interests in seeing a healthy Japan re-emerge, and in keeping that reborn country out of Soviet control, did Korea start to assume significance. However, this evolution of interests was slow to take shape. For most of the 1945–1950 period Americans busied themselves in Korea by being, consecutively, midwife for an artificial state carved out of half a nation, the reluctant foster parent of that state anxious to push it out into the world on its own, and—as tensions worsened around Korea—the halfhearted mentor for a fledgling protege.

U.S. relations with the infant Republic of Korea, inaugurated in August 1945, started off on the wrong foot and grew rapidly worse. The R.O.K.'s first leaders were not so much carefully chosen and installed by a purposeful U.S., as they were the leftover product of a rough-hewn American process of culling undesirable left-wing political claimants. Clearly, some legitimate Korean pretenders to power were culled by poorly informed Americans in the U.S. military government that fostered the R.O.K. Selections were based on a mandate to install a compliant regime capable of becoming viable so the U.S. could shed its onerous tasks in Korea. Though

3

the U.S. preferred another person, Kim Koo, Syngman Rhee's ability to harness Korean nationalism for his own political purposes led to his installation. Washington lacked sufficient capacity and interest to oust Rhee. The result was the creation of a government formed by Syngman Rhee, which quickly became the bane of American authorities.

The elderly Rhee had solid credentials as a patriot, a democrat, and an anti-communist, but often was described as a U.S. puppet. That label barely fit him. Though he was vulnerable to withdrawal of U.S. support, Rhee rarely let that vulnerability deter him from vigorously pressing the U.S. to strengthen its commitment to his agenda for unifying Korea. Often bellicose and obstreperous, Rhee pushed Washington in directions it disliked. Despite American understanding that the Soviet-backed North Korean regime under Kim Il-Sung posed a threat to South Korea, there was little enthusiasm among Americans for declaring the existence of a U.S. national interest in Korean security. Among the least enthusiastic Americans were U.S. military officials who little relished escalating an Asian commitment when the stakes for direct U.S. interests were demonstrably low. Secretary of State Dean Acheson's famous statement, putting Korea outside the scope of the U.S. security frontier in Asia, was in keeping with valid U.S. priorities of the day. Americans were as ambiguous about Korea as Koreans were about the United States.

Not until North Korea's sudden attack, June 25, 1950, was the linkage to the U.S. stake in Japanese interests clearly drawn. Had Japan not been threatened by this move, the U.S. would not have come to the rescue of the R.O.K. The Korean War (or "conflict," since it remained an undeclared war of the nuclear era's "limited war" variety) was, for Koreans, nearly as momentous a turning point for U.S.-Korean relations as the division of the peninsula. For Americans it was far more significant. American support for the R.O.K. accelerated from a crawl to top speed. Where scant interests existed, new-found interests were proclaimed predicated on a U.S. stake in freedom, democracy, and regional peace and security. North Korea's aggression did for South Korea what Rhee failed to do, namely, solidify U.S. support for the R.O.K. By its stealthy attack—it seemed reminiscent to Americans of Pearl Harbor, less than a decade after that infamy—the Kim regime simultaneously drew the U.S. into the war to help an underdog repel communist aggression and gave Pyongyang a sinister image in the American popular consciousness.

Had the U.S. not come to South Korea's aid, the North almost certainly would have conquered the peninsula. Consequently, the U.S. earned the enduring enmity of North Koreans, who had victory snatched from their grasp by a major power that had said Korea was beyond its interests. It won the enduring thanks of those South Koreans who remember that their state could not have survived without costly American help and generosity. Regardless of American motives—pegged to broader regional interests—South Koreans appreciated the results they were able to enjoy. Though South Korean appreciation sometimes has been strained by later American actions or non-actions, it remains a bedrock reality of U.S.-R.O.K. relations.

Once the war was stalemated by a truce in 1953, and the tense border was put in place between the two Korean adversaries, U.S.-Korean relations entered a new phase. U.S. relations with North Korea chilled into a particularly intense version of the worldwide Cold War. The U.S. saw North Korea as an instrument of dangerous communist bloc aggression that had to be deterred. The U.S. chose two approaches. One entailed leaving behind, after the war, a major contingent of U.S. forces in South Korea to guarantee the U.S. commitment to the R.O.K. and train South Korean armed forces to defend themselves. The other entailed a broad program of economic and political support for the R.O.K., to recover from the devastation of the war. That these measures were advocated prior to the war by Syngman Rhee, to enable the R.O.K. to cope with North Korea, was not lost on either Rhee or Americans who dealt with South Korea. Having been vindicated by events, Rhee was in a much stronger position to take advantage of the new post-Korean war American enthusiasm for rebuilding South Korea and keeping it from falling to communism.

During the 1950s U.S. support for the Rhee regime enabled the R.O.K. to make some progress, but it was not a tremendous success story. Rhee was autocratic and cantankerous. He was bent on meeting the challenge of the communist threat and maintaining domestic stability. He did so, but at the expense of political pluralism. Neither was the Confucian Rhee much interested in the mundane affairs of economic nation building. He was content to leave that to his American advisors and their counterparts in the R.O.K. bureaucracy. Though it is difficult for those without first hand memory to understand South Korea's dire socio-economic straits in the late 1950s/early 1960s—those who think primarily of the R.O.K. as a bustling beehive of technocrats and workers—the realities of the late Rhee years were radically different. South Korea was a desperately poor country whose leaders frequently disdained the grinding hard work required to reconstruct their half of Korea. Burdened by poverty, the aftermath of a destructive war, scant economic infrastructure, a small natural resource base, a large and ill-prepared population swollen with refugees displaced from the north during the war, and a faction-ridden leadership plagued by corruption and little aptitude for routine statecraft, the R.O.K. wallowed. Many Americans were pessimistic about South Korea, viewing it as a "basket case" requiring virtually endless support. Some considered such help "pouring money down a rat hole." Nevertheless, geopolitical priorities prevailed and the support grew. Were it not for enormous and steadfast U.S. economic and military support, it is doubtful that South Korea could have survived the postwar period.

North Korea, of course, received no help from its American enemies. Nor did it receive as much support from its Soviet and Chinese backers as the R.O.K. did from the U.S. However, it fared better than South Korea, largely because of the discipline enforced by the totalitarian Kim regime. Though marching to a very different drummer, North Korea fulfilled its early goals more effectively than South Korea. Pyongyang was helped by its smaller population, reservoir of human skills left over from the Japanese era when the north was the industrial heart of colonial Korea, and its much more favorable natural resource base, which attracted Imperial Japan there originally.

By 1960 the U.S. was confronted with discomforting realities in Korea. Its southern protege was not doing well, while the northern adversaries were on their way to recovery and substantial rearmament. The Rhee regime was politically arrogant and inept, alienating its own people by its authoritarianism. The R.O.K was not remotely a U.S. success story, and often was an embarrassment. Thus, when vocal student protesters—with a green light from the R.O.K. military's elites, who worried about the viability of the Rhee regime and its impact on national security—demanded Rhee's ouster, the U.S. assisted in his removal and retirement in Hawaii.

U.S. relations were controversial with the short-lived Chang Myun government that succeeded Rhee. This nine month experiment with democracy received U.S. support, but many critics consider that support lacked the enthusiasm or resources to forestall the military coup which toppled the fledgling government in May 1961. Such criticism seems warranted, if overstated. Washington was diffident with Seoul's democratic government because that regime was so palpably shaky and faction-ridden. Many Americans then (as now) had doubts about the ability of Koreans to make democracy work because their political culture does not enjoy a significant democratic tradition. It was difficult for the U.S. to sort out the players with any degree of confidence. After Rhee, Washington's support for restructuring was strong, but it focused so much on systemic support that Washington appeared lukewarm in its enthusiasm for the claimants to power. It seemed poised for a systemic shakedown, and then the U.S. could reinforce its support for the victor. At the time, despite rumors of unrest in the military, few actually feared a coup because the R.O.K. army was believed to have absorbed enough from U.S. style civil-military relations to preclude that prospect.

Unfortunately, the same freewheeling shakedown process that struck American officials as too tenuous to warrant more discrete support was seen by some in the R.O.K. army as incipient anarchy. Whether these concerns were real, or a pretext for doing what the coupmakers wanted when Rhee was edged out, remains controversial, but—regardless of their real motives—Park Chung-hee and his cohorts staged the R.O.K.'s first military coup. U.S. reaction to that event is poorly understood by most Americans and Koreans. Because of its later support for the Park regime, many critics assume U.S. support stretched back to the regime's founding. Actually, the U.S. was displeased by Park's coup, seeing it as a rejection of the democratic values to which the R.O.K. aspired and for which the U.S. had fought during the Korean War. Making matters worse, the R.O.K. military was widely seen to be a creature of U.S. origin. For this group, so closely identified with Americans, to overthrow the system the U.S. was committed to preserve was a reversal for U.S. policy. Americans on the scene reacted adversely and tried clumsily to abort the coup, but failed. U.S.-R.O.K. relations suffered from this blatant difference of opinion and ill-fated intervention.

Viewing the power Park and his cadre wielded, Washington had no realistic choice other than adjusting to the new regime. However, the adjustment was not smooth and American rationalizations of why the U.S. could support Park as a self-annointed head of the R.O.K. long were strained by questions about his regime's legitimacy. Ambiguity about Korea was revived and strengthened for a new generation of Americans and their policymakers. It was not until the Park junta transformed itself into a "civilian" government in a plausible election, and started to pull the R.O.K. up by its economic bootstraps, that Washington showed any real enthusiasm for Seoul's second wave of leaders. U.S. encouragement for that civilianization process was productive. By the mid-1960s U.S.-R.O.K. relations were on more solid footing, made stronger by Seoul's initial economic successes, its progress in normalizing formal R.O.K.-Japan diplomatic relations, and U.S. concerns that the burgeoning war in Vietnam could leave its commitment in Korea vulnerable to a move by Pyongyang to open a second front. These pressures, and some U.S. acceptance of Park's rationalization that unruly South Koreans require firm leadership, moved Washington toward its own version of normalization with Seoul.

As South Korea prospered under Park's rule, its economy blossomed in ways that were unimaginable to many American advisors. U.S. economic and military aid, and the introduction of Peace Corps volunteers, played a role of which American officials are justifiably proud, but other factors also loomed large. The strengthened economic bonds between Japan and South Korea helped that renaissance, as did the economic by-products of South Korean participation in the Vietnam War. That war played an economic role for South Korea in the late 1960s and early 1970s that replicated the role played by the Korean War for Japan's 1950s economy. By helping the U.S. and South Vietnam, South Korea benefited enormously in both economic and strategic terms. The latter was important to the U.S. because the R.O.K. was the only ally to send a truly large contingent to fight alongside its forces. Though R.O.K. forces were subsidized by the U.S., the image of an Asian ally lending a hand in an unpopular war was invaluable for Washington. Furthermore, this trilateral cooperation in Southeast Asia facilitated continued U.S. support for its Northeast Asian commitments.

This whole arrangement worked reasonably well until the Vietnam experience soured. Despite South Korean efforts to be a reliable ally, and the significant fringe benefits it produced for them, that war proved damaging to its long term relations with the U.S. American setbacks in Indochina raised serious questions about the durability of U.S. resolve in other Asian commitments. The Vietnamization process and the related Nixon (or Guam) Doctrine of encouraging other Asian allies to be more self-reliant in self-defense caused new frictions in U.S.-R.O.K. relations. U.S. forces in Korea were cut by 20,000 under President Nixon. If South Korea could afford to send some of its forces off to war in Vietnam, and still cope with North Korea, logic suggested it could suffice with a smaller number of U.S. forces when its own forces returned. Moreover, the newly battle-hardened R.O.K. forces now had an experiential advantage which their North Korean foes lacked. In addition, even its early economic successes made the R.O.K. more capable of paying for such self-reliance. Finally, U.S. popular support for Asian authoritarian regimes with uncertain domestic political legitimacy raised new doubts about undesirable spillover from Indochina to Korea. Park's 1970s crackdown on domestic critics and his notorious Yushin constitution intensified those concerns.

Seoul reacted adversely to these developments. Aware that North Korea could be tempted by diluted U.S. support for South Korea, and that Pyongyang was stressed by the Sino-Soviet split and

Beijing's cultural revolution, Seoul worried greatly about continued U.S. support. North Korea intensified this concern by periodically engaging in hostile acts against South Korea and—less frequently— U.S. forces defending it. Though these hostile acts reinforced American perceptions of the dangers in Korea, they also underscored the dangers of American involvement in another Asian war. Park's concern about Washington's reactions exacerbated his domestic political crackdowns. His efforts to compel domestic stability aggravated the uncertainties behind U.S. support for his regime. Besides overt appeals for support, Seoul engaged during the early 1970s in covert efforts to influence U.S. policy toward Korea that ultimately produced the damaging "Koreagate" investigation.

When the U.S. departed Vietnam in the mid-1970s, the legacy of that war left a strong imprint on U.S. relations with all other Asian states. South Korean officials were especially nervous because the R.O.K. faced the most imminent threat. The election of Jimmy Carter, who had campaigned—in part—on commitments to emphasize human rights and to reassess the U.S. troop presence in Korea, cast a pall over U.S.-R.O.K. relations. That cloud intensified as Carter tried to keep those promises, as trade frictions emerged, and as the controversy surrounding Koreagate exacerbated mutual antagonisms. Though Carter's human rights campaign raised the hopes of South Korean opposition and dissident leaders, it ultimately produced more heat than light. U.S. and R.O.K. reassessments of the North Korean threat led Washington to halt its anticipated cutbacks. The strategic arguments used successfully to counter Carter's troop cutback plans also undercut the human rights issue. South Korean "national security" became an instrument for tempering both reform efforts. The dangers of pressing Park so hard that he would go the way of the Shah and Somosa proved too threatening to what were deemed larger U.S. interests in regional peace and stability. Similar arguments about costs and benefits also minimized the early trade disputes, graphic symbols of yet another wave of U.S. ambiguity about the proper American policy towards Korea. Washington had several desirable goals in mind, but substantial uncertainty about what priorities should be accorded them.

The assassination of President Park on October 26, 1979, the result of domestic upheavals and internecine squabbling within the Seoul leadership, at first seemed a blessing in disguise because it might introduce a more pluralistic political milieu. Though many feared chaos would again tempt Pyongyang to strike, nothing happened. South Koreans reacted calmly, anxious to get on with their lives and business. Instead of disorder, the leaders of the South Korean body politic coalesced into rival camps led by the "Three Kims" (Kim Dae-jung, Kim Yong-sam, and Kim Jong-pil) who entered a heated quest for the presidency. In the wake of an intra-military coup and partial purge led by General Chun Doo-hwan, launched December 12, 1979, the military pledged to stand aside and ensure that political processes would work freely. It was widely assumed that Park's heir apparent and architect of his 1961 coup, Kim Jong-pil, would emerge victorious. Given the apprehension about turmoil after Park, this prospect—if it resulted from an open process—was reassuring to many Americans.

A not-so-funny event happened on the way to the ballot box. While most Americans were preoccupied with the chaos surrounding the Iran hostage situation, convulsive events erupted in South Korea. Amid strident electoral campaigning and opposition rhetoric that broached normally taboo ideological issues, riot control forces vigorously put down demonstrations. In counterreaction, protests spread—including to Kwangju in May 1980—where they burgeoned into a massive and popularly supported insurrection. Because Kwangju is the center of Kim Dae-jung's home province (Cholla), linkages were drawn and lines demarcated. Chun dispatched R.O.K. armed forces to quell the unrest by exceptionally violent actions. Because of the unusual command structure in Korea, where the senior U.S. general also heads the "Combined Forces Command," R.O.K. forces may—in the event of war—be under U.S. leadership. Consequently there were widespread, but unwarranted, allegations that the U.S. either sanctioned or did not try to stop Chun from suppressing the Kwangju unrest. Those Korean forces used in Kwanju were emphatically not under American control. Because many died (estimates vary from about 190 to over 2,000), this event—a turning point in Chun's seizure of power—is, nonetheless, seen by many South Koreans as particularly egregious evidence of U.S. complicity with authoritarian rule in Seoul. Despite widespread, and vigorous, U.S. denials, the circumstances surrounding the Kwangju incident have haunted U.S.-R.O.K. relations and provided invaluable leverage for North Korean propagandists.

During the rest of 1980 Chun manipulated the political system, shunted the three Kims aside, and emerged atop the heap. As Seoul's elites were sorting out the post-Kwangju turmoil, Americans selected their most conservative leader in decades. Though not directly linked to events in Seoul, Reagan's victory made more feasible Chun's eventual succession. Had Carter won a second term, Chun might have reconsidered his plans. With Reagan enroute to the White House, however, South Korean national security-based arguments and rationales were guaranteed a more receptive audience. General Chun Doo-hwan's preliminary intra-military coup in the fall of 1979, his political moves during 1980–81, and questionable election in March 1981 by an electoral college dominated by his forces, clearly sealed South Korea's political fate. Through a very different sort of prolonged coup, General Chun had, no less than General Park, seized power with R.O.K. army backing.

Though there was much short-term American popular criticism of Chun's actions, the positive reaction of the Reagan administration contrasted sharply with the U.S. reactions in 1961 to Park's coup. Far from being critical, Chun was warmly embraced. His welcome to Washington by the Reagan administration, as the first visiting major head of state, put an implicit stamp of approval on the Chun regime, buying it a level of acceptance in international and South Korean circles that it otherwise lacked. Chun's government was delirious at the turn of events. Jokes circulated in Seoul that Chun was black-and-blue from pinching himself to be sure this was really happening to him. Seoul's new leader now had a strong supportive counterpart in Washington and the future looked bright.

During the years in which Chun and Reagan overlapped, U.S.-R.O.K. relations officially were better than they had ever been. South Korea's confidence in the U.S. commitment to Korea seemingly was at a new high, U.S.-R.O.K. economic ties blossomed so that U.S. economic and military aid were no longer necessary and were terminated, and, for most of the period, U.S. tolerance for Seoul's political excesses was great indeed. However, during this same period (1981–87) tensions continued, usually beneath the surface. The specifics of these tensions concern contemporary U.S.-R.O.K. security, economic, and political prospects and their regional setting, addressed in subsequent sections. However, it is worth suggesting their place in the grand continuum of U.S.-Korean relations. The confluence of two strongly anti-communist governments in Seoul and Washington produced a new wave of mutual empathy at the official level. However, this empathy for each other was so strong that much real controversy was swept under the rug in the interest of maintaining the newfound harmony. In a sense, the Reagan-Chun coterminous years produced an artificial moratorium, keeping a lid on many tensions and deflecting tough decisions.

President Reagan's visit to Seoul in November 1983, reciprocating Chun's 1981 trip, was widely interpreted by Seoul officials and media as symbolic of a new age of "reciprocity," "mutual interdependence," and an "inseparable partnership." Such rhetoric was standard fare during the Reagan-Chun years. As diplomatic rhetoric it is understandable, but—taken seriously, as many in the Reagan and Chun administrations appeared to do—it obfuscates some serious problems that linger from the 1950s, 60s, and 70s. The U.S.-R.O.K. relationship is tempered by some degree of R.O.K. dependency. That relationship is also troubled by mutual stereotypes and ambivalence. The love/hate bonds are alive and well. Moreover, the numerous problems arising from a divided Korean nation make rhetoric about real reciprocity or interdependency farfetched.

Against that background, several major themes are examined in this study. Instead of a steady convergence toward common national interests, substantial converging interests may tug against equally substantial diverging interests. This is a sign of mature U.S.-R.O.K. relations, reflecting growth and change on both sides. Once the moratorium Chun/Reagan years are past, these differences are likely to be more visible. These include the internationalization of the

R.O.K., the broadening of the D.P.R.K.'s horizons, and the re-Asianization of both Koreas. These trends are complicated by the enduring realities of grossly uneven knowledge and understanding of each other among Americans and Koreans. Many South Koreans are reasonably familiar with things American and a large group of government officials, academics, and businessmen are expert in such matters. Conversely, very few Americans know much about Korea, the U.S. cadre of Korea experts pales in comparison to their Korean counterpart experts in U.S. affairs, and most average Americans know little about Korea, and care less. The only real exception to that rule was the popularity of the M*A*S*H television show which spread misinformation to the masses for years. South Korea's place in overall U.S. foreign policy—while improved after decades of American involvement—remained remarkably derivative of other U.S. interests in Asian and world affairs. Against this summary of some forty years of mixed postwar U.S. relations with Korea, we shall turn to key U.S. areas of concern: contemporary security, economic, political, and regional relations.

2 Key Issues in Contemporary U.S.-Korean Relations

Contemporary United States relations with the Republic of Korea and Democratic People's Republic of Korea are complex. Four key issue areas set the stage for the topics covered in this study's recommendations. These issues are treated in accordance with the priority normally assigned to them by Washington—security, economic, political, and regional affairs.

Security Relations

In early 1987, Assistant Secretary of Defense Richard Armitage said that the U.S. and R.O.K. were "about to embark on a new security partnership." He optimistically said "In only a few decades [South Koreans] have transformed a nation that was completely dependent upon the U.S. military presence into a self-confident, newly industrialized country that is capable of assuming most of the cost of its own defense."

Those cogent remarks were in keeping with the post-Vietnam War tendency of U.S. policymakers to reassure the R.O.K. at every opportunity of its continued support and to express appreciation for all that South Korea does militarily. Recent U.S. Ambassadors to Korea have repeatedly described U.S. security interests in Korea as "vital." Then Secretary of Defense Weinberger came closer to the mark when he, in 1986, told R.O.K. Defense Minister Yi Ki-baek that Korean security is "pivotal to the peace and stability of Northeast Asia, which in turn is vital to the security of the United States."

The Reagan administration has effectively defused South Korean security fears growing out of the Carter troop cutback proposals and talk of a U.S. "swing strategy" which would have shifted U.S.

forces from Asia to Europe in a crisis. Washington and Seoul, with justification, proclaim new levels of bilateral strategic cooperation. That cooperation assumed new, if temporary, significance in 1988 as the U.S. commitment to South Korea encompassed responsibilities to assure peace during the Seoul Olympics.

U.S. reassurances to Seoul also go far beyond words. During the 1980s a number of major American arms transfers to South Korea occurred. These enabled the R.O.K. to quantitatively and qualitatively improve its forces' capabilities. This was part of the R.O.K.'s Force Improvement Plan (F.I.P.) measures begun in response to initial post-Vietnam qualms about U.S. support. By far the most controversial episode concerned Washington's 1981 policy reversal that fostered the sale of F-16s to South Korea. Though this strengthened the R.O.K., it also raised the ante in the North-South arms race and may have helped cause the subsequent expansion in Soviet military aid to North Korea. Other signals of a strengthened U.S. commitment include the 1986 decision to deploy newer weapons systems like the medium-range "Lance" missiles to replace the obsolescing "Honest John" and "Sergeant" missiles previously in the U.S. inventory in Korea. The potential nuclear capability of the Lance was readily noted in Korea.

U.S. pressures on South Korea to contribute a fairer share of security costs, more commensurate with the R.O.K.'s new economic resources, produced the Combined Defense Improvement Plan (C.D.I.P.). This is a device by which South Korea is scheduled to contribute to the upkeep of U.S. forces in Korea. Seoul's annual F.I.P.s and C.D.I.P.s have strengthened South Korean forces and U.S.-R.O.K. cooperation. Both also were greatly aided by the rapid expansion of South Korea's arms production capabilities. Despite these factors, South Korea rarely lets an opportunity pass to underscore to the U.S. that more needs to be done.

Differing Security Perspectives

Despite the emphasis Washington and Seoul place on U.S.-R.O.K. strategic harmony, there are significant differences between the allies. As a superpower, the U.S. necessarily must think in much broader and complex terms about the North Korean and Soviet threats than South Korea does. Typically South Koreans hold much more localized and parochial attitudes toward the Soviet Union's threat to the R.O.K. There is little sense in Seoul that Soviet forces pose a direct threat to South Korea and less understanding of the Soviet-North Korean strategic implications for the U.S. as seen by Americans.

Because Seoul's view of the North Korean threat is much narrower than Washington's perspective, South Koreans tend to accept actually using joint conventional deterrence forces against North Korea. Americans tend to be more reluctant. Consequently, the prospect of waging war in Korea—while far more real for Koreans— is less terrifying and more feasible for South Koreans than for Americans. Such a conflict has broader significance to Americans. Another Korean war could too easily escalate to nuclear war, that could draw in the Soviets, for Americans to be comfortable with the prospect of actually fighting it. Few Americans can visualize a superpower either winning or surviving a nuclear war. This prospect also strongly influences neighboring Japan's threat perceptions, reinforcing its reluctance to get involved in Korean affairs. Because of this different perspective on war as an abstraction and a reality, Americans and South Koreans hold different threat perceptions and fears of war. This makes their attitudes toward war in Korea equally different.

Stemming from these differences are markedly dissimilar attitudes toward opposite ends of the strategic question in Korea: tension-reduction and the R.O.K.'s nuclear options. The prospects for real arms reduction and tension control in contemporary Korea are considered by most American and South Korean officials to be guarded at best. Because of the discord surrounding the repeated failures of North and South Korea to achieve reunification, and their uncertain commitment to that elusive goal, neither Korea has been particularly serious about tension-reduction or confidence-building measures. Exacerbating this situation is a tendency of Koreans to be confrontational and pugnacious in conflicts. Washington generally goes along with Seoul on security issues, but U.S. global interests in such local measures are far stronger than

South Korea's. Moreover, Americans are more prone than Koreans to compromise in conflict situations. Consequently, the potential for a meaningful U.S. initiative toward tension-reduction or confidence-building measures in Korea is much greater than for a comparable South Korean initiative.

One possibility for reducing tensions is the nuclear issue. North Korea and the Soviet Union often press for reduction or elimination of the U.S. "nuclear umbrella" protecting South Korea. Their support for variations of the nuclear-free zone approach clearly is aimed at undercutting the U.S. security commitment to the R.O.K. For obvious reasons, comparable to NATO arrangements, the U.S. is not prepared to fold its umbrella, nor does Seoul favor that option. However, nuclear weapons seriously complicate the U.S.-R.O.K. security relationship. As much as the U.S. might like to pursue reduced tensions in Korea, its interests in preserving deterrence in Northeast Asia damage the prospects.

In a sense the U.S. does not enjoy a choice in the matter, because the R.O.K.'s (and Japan's) independent nuclear options are real. As the 1978 Congressional hearings on U.S.-R.O.K. relations showed, Seoul decided to develop nuclear weapons in the early 1970s when its confidence in the U.S. was shaken. American pressures and reassurances dissuaded Seoul, but the option remains available to it. Despite periodic disavowals of such intentions, South Korea does have the potential to become a small nuclear power. The destabilizing implications for regional proliferation and security are severe, giving Seoul implicit leverage over U.S. policy. Perversely, South Korea has its own fears about the nuclear issue. As much as the R.O.K. needs the U.S. nuclear umbrella, the notion that nuclear weapons may be more readily used in Korea than in other parts of the world scares many South Koreans. Seoul welcomes the show of U.S. commitment, but dreads "winning" a war against North Korea if that means inflicting limited nuclear devastation on other Koreans and then having to live next door to the consequences forever.

Another major disruptive element in U.S.-R.O.K. security relations is the proper role for U.S. and R.O.K. forces, and arrangements within the Combined Forces Command. U.S. domination of the military hierarchy has grated on South Korean nationalistic sensibilities for years. Since most forces defending the R.O.K. are South Korean, not American, the U.S.-led hierarchy affronts many Koreans. Perpetuating these awkward arrangements maintains the geopolitical fig leaf of the United Nation's presence, the bureaucratic necessity of American forces in any foreign joint command being under a U.S. commander, and Seoul's desire to reinforce the broad array of U.S. force deployments which the R.O.K. sees as its "tripwire." However, these arrangements are under increasing criticism within South Korea because they are incongruous in a proudly nationalistic, prosperous, and nearly self-reliant ally. Furthermore, they inaccurately give the impression in Korea and abroad that the U.S.-led security system sanctions the sometimes repressive internal political arrangements in Seoul.

Economic Relations

U.S. economic relations with the Koreas are almost entirely with South Korea. Americans are constrained from trading with North Korea by a U.S. trade embargo and COCOM restrictions on trade with communist states. U.S. relations with North Korea are so dismal that scant opportunity exists for the development of trade. Reinforcing that predisposition is the relatively low status of the North Korean economy compared to the South Korean, which has approximately five times the North's G.N.P. Pyongyang's credit rating is virtually nil. It has defaulted on numerous debts and never repaid outstanding principal on foreign loans.

In contrast, the South Korean economy's success story is renowned. Annual per capita income grew from about $80, when Park Chung-hee seized power, and $150 in the mid-1960s, to over $2,300 in 1987. Though the R.O.K.'s debt burden went from about $8.5 billion in the late 1970s to over $40 billion in 1987, South Korean leaders and technocrats have no serious problems meeting the payments on the debt or sustaining economic growth. More important, that debt is now being reduced. The growth rate of the R.O.K. economy has been relatively high, even when other countries

19

experienced slumps, and has been ten percent or better for long periods during its booms.

Despite problems, Seoul remains emphatically bullish on its economic prospects. With a 12.5% growth rate in G.N.P. in 1986, and 12.2% in 1987; and $34 billion in exports in 1986 (including a trade surplus with the U.S. of $7.4 billion) and $46 billion in 1987 (including a $10 billion trade surplus with the U.S.), Seoul is confident. The 1987 performance came despite major political and labor unrest. South Korea has reason to believe that its Sixth Five-Year Plan (1987-1991) can overcome problems as effectively as earlier plans did. Despite problems in the international economic environment, Seoul—as of late 1987—expected the R.O.K. economy to grow 8.5% in real terms during 1988. Furthermore, South Korean leaders are confident the Seoul Olympics will help accelerate the R.O.K.'s economic success.

Since the mid-1980s, South Korea has become a more visible economic presence on the U.S. scene. By 1986 it had displaced France as the United States' seventh ranking trade partner. Also during the 1980s South Korea became a small, but growing, investment presence in the U.S. South Korea hoped—like Japan—to hedge its bets against U.S. protectionist pressures by fostering so-called "transplants." These innovations made it more difficult for the R.O.K. to retain its formal status as a developing country protected by provisions of the G.A.T.T. which enable it to avoid exposing its vulnerabilities to free competition from other countries. These circumstances made it difficult for the U.S. to respond as strongly as some advocates of protectionist retaliation desired, despite data showing the U.S. in 1986 provided about a 40% market share for South Korean exports. This large market share provides an invaluable base upon which R.O.K. industries build economies of scale, and profits, that enable them to compete in other export markets. Americans selling to South Korea lacked comparable advantages or access. American awareness of South Korea's competitive ability increased greatly as a result of what the Washington Post labeled a "Korean import flood."

At about that juncture one of South Korea's advertising agencies published ads for itself which were more symbolic than it presumably intended. They proclaimed: "Hey look! The new kid on the block is all grown up." That imagery was premature for it and the R.O.K. However, it conveyed the feelings of many Americans toward South Korea. It was no longer a pliant protege. As one book title put it, the U.S.-R.O.K. economic relationship was rapidly shifting "from patron to partner," but it was an inequitable partnership.

Trade Frictions

South Korea in the 1980s appeared to be joining Japan as an economic rival of the United States. South Korean economic leaders like Nam Duck-woo (Chairman of the Korean Traders Association) and Rha Woong-bae (Minister of Economic Planning), are adamant that the R.O.K is not a Japanese clone and to treat it so is unfair, and exacerbates trans-Pacific trade frictions. They cite the structural differences in the two Asian economies; severe strategic pressures felt by the R.O.K. economy, unlike Japan's; South Korea's flexibility and more cooperative attitudes toward the U.S.; and the significantly smaller scale of South Korea's economy compared to the gargantuan Japanese economy. Though most American trade specialists, and those working on Korean affairs, are happy to concede these points to Seoul's spokesmen, the parallels between the Japanese and South Korean economic models remain a major factor contributing to U.S. economic policy toward Korea.

Seoul's disavowals are more than a bit disingenous. South Korea's economic development is based on an export-led, labor-intensive, import-dependent, low-wage, military-influenced, oligarchical, and authoritarian system rooted in the Confucian values it shares with Japan. Moreover, many South Korean leaders of the economic renaissance had either first hand experience as entrepreneurs under colonial Japan or imbibed the Japanese experience during the colonial era. Collectively, these factors, coupled with Japan's major role in stimulating the South Korean economy during the late 1960s and 1970s, after Japan-R.O.K. diplomatic relations were established in 1965, made a dramatic impact on the structure and performance of South Korea's economy.

The Reagan Administration hoped to minimize trade frictions with South Korea. But many other American voices expressed very different aims. Despite repeated promises by Seoul to really improve trade relations, and some limited moves, the U.S. business community in Korea remained angry about what it viewed as discrimination from the R.O.K. bureaucracy and halfhearted pressures for reform from Washington. In the U.S., too, there are signs that American patience is growing short and tempers are rising.

Aside from sluggish American efforts, the primary explanations for the lack of progress in increasing U.S. exports to Korea lie in R.O.K. bureaucratic inertia and footdragging. Seoul ballyhoos its high rate (93.6%) of import liberalization as a sign that its markets are being opened. However, Seoul's use of non-tariff barriers, bureaucratic taxing and inspection devices, banking regulations, and encouragement of culturally based Korean preferences cumulatively undermines most of the gains it ostensibly has achieved. In such circumstances, it is little wonder that Americans do not try harder to penetrate the South Korean market.

Precisely at a point in 1987 when South Korea was being rocked by wave after wave of political and labor unrest, it also had to face the prospect of intensified U.S. pressures to address trade complaints. The combination of U.S. domestic economic problems—symbolized by the October 1987 stock market crash—and the start of the lengthy run up to the 1988 U.S. presidential election campaign, in which trade policy was a factor, promised to compel Washington to adopt more tough-minded economic policies at home and abroad. Few doubted Washington had to rectify U.S. economic problems, but there was no sure sign what would be done or when it would occur. Seoul grew noticeably nervous as it looked to the future of U.S.-Korean economic ties. Accentuating its anxiety was a tendency of the South Korean public to react to U.S. pressures in a xenophobic, nationalistic manner. Since the mid-1980s, South Korea officials have variously complained about American callousness, complacency, arrogance, laziness, and lack of empathy for Korean problems. These feelings are still powerful in South Korea, contributing to anti-American sentiments among elites and masses. However, because Seoul recognizes its ultimate weaknesses in negotiating with the U.S., most South Korean critics of American economic policies have toned down their remarks.

Since mid-1987, South Korea experienced serious new U.S. efforts to get it to reduce more of its tariffs on U.S. products; to place new emphasis on opening Korean markets to high-tech U.S. products; and to open its markets to American competition at an accelerated pace, shortening the schedule for market liberalization by one year. Washington also pressured Seoul to crack down on black market exports of counterfeit brandname products; to stop trying to expand its third party arms sales in competition with U.S. weapons producers; and to expand South Korean investments in the United States. U.S. Trade Representative, Clayton Yeutter, in December 1987 explained these pressures, "I probably get more letters today complaining about Korean trade practices than I do any other country in the world." U.S. rhetoric became harsher, but its actions remained restrained for fear of destabilizing South Korea at a time of political uncertainty.

Because South Koreans are perennially anxious about the durability of their new prosperity, their ability to repay their massive debts if their economy falters, and the broader significance for U.S.-R.O.K. geopolitical ties should currency and trade strains damage other economic ties, they have been somewhat more forthcoming. The R.O.K. made a major effort to advertise its policies and improve its image in the United States in 1987. The centerpiece of that campaign was a R.O.K. government-backed buying mission to the U.S., to purchase $2.6 billion worth of American goods and make Americans more aware that there are potential customers in Korea for U.S. products. The Roh Tae-woo government, starting in early 1988, stepped up Seoul's efforts to get South Koreans to buy more American products, despite domestic opposition to South Korea bowing to American demands for market-opening concessions.

Seoul also used international forums to press its case that protectionism is dangerous, making the case to Washington that the U.S., too, would be hurt by any restrictions it might impose on trade with Asia. Bolstered by the voices of Americans who support free trade in the interests of the United States, these concrete efforts enjoyed some success. The effectiveness of South Korea's major lobbying efforts in the U.S. is much less certain. Its use of large lobbying firms, prominent Americans, and—indirectly—media and academic spinoffs from the Rev. Moon's organization, which often act as de facto voices for South Korean interests, have not paid noticeable political dividends. The voices of pro-R.O.K. Americans who are not employed by Seoul seem more effective, but this is difficult to measure. Against the background of Koreagate, Seoul routinely runs the risk of its direct economic lobbying backfiring politically, once again.

Political Relations

While the South Korean economy long ago reached the take-off stage and is now a high flier, the South Korean political system still is thumping along a pothole-ridden runway searching for its take-off stage and trying not to crash. Stretching this metaphor, the R.O.K. political system has far too many would-be pilots and too few people willing to be cooperative crew members or to go along for the ride. South Korean politics is plagued by too much authoritarianism and factionalism. Though there are many who cloak themselves in the mantle of "democracy," there is little South Korean appreciation for the give-and-take processes essential in a functioning democracy.

Widespread American skepticism about the prospects for a thriving democracy in South Korea is warranted. Nonetheless, the U.S. is hopeful that democracy will sink deep roots in Korea and flourish. Its support for democracy has remained relatively constant despite many reversals. However, facilitating democratic pluralism often is a no-win, damned-if-you-do/damned-if-you-don't, task for the U.S. If it is too outspoken or forceful in pressing its interests, it runs the risk of being perceived as manipulative and "imperial." If it is low-key, it risks being seen as indifferent toward democracy or supportive of dictatorship. In either case, U.S. actions can feed anti-Americanism. During much of the 1980s the Reagan administration was widely criticized for the alleged ineffectiveness of its "quiet diplomacy" and very low profile human rights policies. Ambassador Richard ("Dixie") Walker drew especially strong criticism from U.S. and Korean human rights activists, though a plausible case can be made that his rapport with the Chun government tempered its worst political excesses.

An indicator of how bad broad U.S.-R.O.K. political relations became in the Reagan-Chun years was the intensification of South Korean anti-Americanism. In an inverse relationship, as Washington and Seoul proclaimed vastly improved political harmony, popular South Korean feelings toward the U.S. deteriorated seriously. Anti-Americanism was evident in hostile comments by opposition politicians and human rights activists about Ambassador Walker and his successor, James Lilley, various senior U.S. military officials, and Washington officials. Alleged U.S. support for Chun during Kwangju, and obvious support for him as president, cast the U.S. in a negative role. Attacks on non-military U.S. Government facilities in the R.O.K. followed, with threats and hostile attitudes toward individual Americans. The early and mid Reagan-Chun years gave anti-Americanism a legitimacy and scope in South Korean society which it had never enjoyed previously. Economic frictions added fuel to these fires. On a few occasions, the Chun government shortsightedly fanned these fires to enhance its leverage in domestic politics and in its trade ties with the U.S. A notable example was the 1985 controversy over U.S. imposition of restrictions on the export of South Korean photo albums to the U.S., which Seoul vocally alleged was a gratuitous American attack on low paid Korean workers.

Anti-Chun sentiments and anti-Americanism coalesced at a high level in mid-1987 when the South Korean political situation boiled over, scalding American interests in the process. Though some American officials have been cavalier about the seriousness of anti-Americanism in Korea, there seems little doubt that it is profound and could be damaging to the U.S. stake in Korea and Northeast Asia. The Shultz-Sigur team at the Department of State tried to take the edge off anti-Americanism by signaling Washington's hope that Chun would keep his word to guide the R.O.K. through a peaceful transfer of power. Dr. Gaston Sigur, Assistant Secretary of State for East Asia, took the lead in that effort by publicly laying out U.S. expectations for the post-Chun era in a major speech before the U.S.-Korea Society in February 1987. South Korean politics experienced several crises during 1987, beginning with Chun's April moves to change the rules of the game. His subsequent effort to install Roh Tae-woo as heir apparent blew the lid off the pressure cooker he had created.

Throughout the spring and summer South Korea was traumatized by violent political unrest. Several U.S. officials played a discreet, behind-the-scenes, role in ameliorating the tensions. However it was Roh's decisive role in offering political concessions that turned an ugly situation around. Against the background of reassurances of American support for whatever pluralistic political processes the ruling Democratic Justice Party and opposition parties could cobble together, a revised constitution was crafted and approved in time for the December 1987 elections. The election campaign proved predictably factionalized. The two rival Kims (Kim Dae-jung and Kim Yong-sam) in the major opposition party—the Reunification Democratic Party—were unable to remain even remotely unified. Kim Dae-jung defected to run his own bid for the presidency, under the banner of his Peace and Democracy Party. Further complicating the political scene, President Park's former heir apparent, Kim Jong-pil, also jumped into the fray. This reset the stage for the political struggle that was aborted in 1980, with the addition of Roh Tae-woo as a new heir apparent.

The U.S. pointedly tried to keep a low profile in the campaign. The only deviation from that agenda was the September 1987 meeting between Roh and President Reagan when Roh visited Washington. The White House emphasized Mr. Reagan's willingness also to meet with any of the other R.O.K. candidates, but the apparent U.S. support for Roh was used for political purposes by all sides in the campaign. Roh tried to bask subtly in President Reagan's blessing, while his opponents sought to tag him as someone who needed U.S. support.

In any event, the U.S. managed to avoid becoming unduly entangled in the R.O.K. elections. Once Roh Tae-woo became South Korea's president, however, the United States reacted with cautious optimism. Roh's margin of victory—36% to Kim Yong-sam's 28%, Kim Dae-jung's 27%, and Kim Jong-pil's 8%—was larger than anticipated. The pre-election forecasts by Kim Yong-sam and Kim Dae-jung that Roh could only win by fraud were reinforced by post-election complaints about rigging and manipulation. Supporters of the two Kims briefly took to the streets again immediately in the wake of the election to try to reverse the decision, but failed. Though protests against Roh will continue, the cause of the dissident opposition groups was seriously hurt by the election numbers. The two Kims, collectively, won a 55% majority. Had they worked together, instead of splitting egotistically, their side could have claimed victory. Roh did not divide their ranks; they did.

Moreover, had the ruling DJP seriously tampered with the election results, it would have created a firmer margin of victory—presumably a majority, or much more comfortable plurality. Roh's 36% plurality, with an 89% voter turnout, means only 32% of the total South Korean electorate voted for him. Consequently, while the two Kims' grousing must be characterized as "sour grapes," the Roh administration must govern South Korean society from a politically weak base. Accepting such skewed results may be relatively easy in societies with a long democratic tradition. In such societies the electorate often has so much confidence in the established system that voters who abstain from the process, or lose, do not complain when a minority determines the victor. South Korea has no confidence cushion and must cope with some degree of disillusionment when a high ratio of the electorate votes, yet feels disenfranchised when a political minority's choice prevails.

Fortunately, Roh signalled flexibility during his campaign when he said, "It is not desirable to form a cabinet only with pro-DJP people," and "I oppose the winner-take-all formula" in democracy. If Confucian societies, like Korea, have difficulty reconciling themselves to the so-called "tyranny of the majority" in Western-style democracy, they have more problems with sustaining a "tyranny of the plurality." If the Roh government is to avoid serious political upheavals that could damage the image—and perhaps the security—of the 1988 Olympics, it must come to terms with the dissident opposition elements. Given the problems all sides have experienced with achieving compromise, fulfilling this goal may prove difficult. One can only hope that South Korean aspirations that the Seoul Olympics can be a unifying factor will be fulfilled. They do have reason for such hopes because the Olympics promise to be a rallying point for South Korean national pride which could draw together Koreans of disparate political views.

Washington has high hopes about the future of democracy in South Korea now that the major hurdle of Seoul's first peaceful electoral transfer of power has been overcome. The Reagan administration's sighs of relief that the election took place peacefully and was not blocked by the military, were virtually audible throughout the tense months of late 1987. However, the fear of military intervention did not disappear simply because the election was held successfully and Roh won. South Korean politics remain subject to a military veto. Roh's military background reduces, but does not eliminate, the risks of another coup.

The thinly veiled warnings of some military leaders about the prospect of Kim Dae-jung as president were symbolic of a broader willingness of many in the military elite to bear ultimate responsibility for South Korean well-being and stability. Any politician who puts either factor in jeopardy runs the risk of another military crackdown. Should serious political unrest resurface under President Roh, those in the military who see themselves as the guarantors of the R.O.K.'s survival can be expected to be acutely interested. In their own way, politically motivated South Korean military leaders consider themselves to be more dedicated to national well being than patriotic dissidents, who see themselves as a bulwark against militarism. It is in Roh's interest to mollify the military's concerns and discreetly involve as many of them as possible in decision-making so that they will feel a sense of responsibility for his success.

The Roh government must cope with a delicate balancing act. Simultaneously, Roh must reassure the military that he has its best interests at heart and convince his opponents that his government is not a military regime. He has to prove that he is not a "militarist" or "dictator," and put some distance between himself and the military. However, he cannot afford to alienate the military in the process. Further complicating this potential for military problems is the question of how to respond to the perceived societal needs of Korean Military Academy classes which graduated in the 1960s and '70s. They will be denied a chance at power if the R.O.K. army's political influence is deflected. This group may be frustrated by the foreclosure of political opportunities open to previous KMA classes. Roh, a member of the famous KMA 11th class, may have a difficult time convincing successive classes to stay out of politics. Roh confronts the awkward task of bringing into his government enough of the next KMA generation to mollify them, while not reinforcing his regime's military legacy.

The role of the Olympics is ambiguous in shaping the prospects of another coup. Given a choice between successfully holding the Olympics under a regime led by politicians troubled by continued unrest, or intervening in politics to insure the stability many in the military prefer and risk losing the Olympics, one cannot be confident the high price of armed intervention could deter determined military activists. Furthermore, after the Olympics, advocates of military intervention may be less inhibited. Of all the near-term dangers in South Korean politics, this is the one that most concerns U.S. interests. Washington has been crystal-clear in its opposition to any more coups or martial law in Korea. If either occurs despite many U.S. signals that it could jeopardize U.S.-R.O.K. relations, Washington would have a profound problem on its hands.

Regional Affairs

The two Koreas have achieved a rough equilibrium with the major powers. South Korea enjoys strong support from the U.S. and the indirect support of Japan. North Korea enjoys moderate support from both China and the Soviet Union. Though South Korea experiments with overtures toward the P.R.C., the U.S.S.R., Vietnam, and the eastern European states, and North Korea does so with Japan and—to a lesser extent—the U.S., little movement has occurred. Seoul harbors palpable hopes that the 1988 Olympics will stimulate improved R.O.K.-P.R.C. ties. It also harbors ambitious but somewhat forlorn hopes that R.O.K.-U.S.S.R. ties might be improved by Olympic contacts. Under President Chun, South Korea experimented with two foreign affairs approaches borrowed

29

from Japan: omnidirectional foreign policy and the separation of politics from economics in international affairs. President Roh is accelerating their use. In contrast to the Rhee and Park eras, Roh's foreign policy is much more flexible toward communist states. With the important exceptions of its policies toward North Korea and regarding domestic politics, South Korea no longer is the arch-hardline anti-communist state it once was.

North Korea worries about these prospects as much as South Korea relishes them. It is uncertain how Beijing, Moscow, and other communist capitals will respond to this opportunity. Pyongyang's responses are cause for greater concern for fear that North Korea may attempt to disrupt the games, directly or indirectly. Consequently, all sides await the 1988 Summer Olympics with great anticipation and some apprehension.

On balance, however, all the major powers are reasonably content with the Korean status quo, predicated on the perpetuation of a divided Korea. This reality contradicts official backing of all the major powers in the region for the various unification proposals proffered by the half of Korea with which they are friendly. This is the crux of contemporary U.S. policy toward inter-Korean relations: does Washington support Seoul's position and desire unification? The answer today remains an ambiguous "yes and no," it supports Seoul but not unification.

Official Washington would answer "yes" to both halves of that query, but the answer is a diplomatic obfuscation. To say "yes" to both suggests that U.S. support for any of Seoul's unification positions equates with support for real reunification. That, unfortunately, is a false supposition because none of Seoul's past or present proposals for unification have had a real chance and both Seoul and Washington know it. The U.S. normally supports the R.O.K.'s unification proposals and often sounds enthusiastic about them, but that position actually supports a process that is almost certain to remain stalemated indefinitely. Hence, U.S. support really is support for the status quo of a divided Korea, not for the prospect of a unified Korea.

There is no sign that this situation is likely to change soon through the actions of either Korean state. Each Korea always inserts some sort of "Catch-22" obstacle into its proposals that is certain to provoke a rejection by the other Korea. Not until both Koreas are willing to drop these tactics and enter negotiations, can any change from the contemporary stalemate be anticipated. Despite glimmers of hope that the 1988 Olympics would induce serious tension-reduction in Korea, it has not come to pass.

So far, appropriate pretexts have always arisen to wreck all talks. Most incidents have been provoked by North Korea, giving the R.O.K. and U.S. every right to believe that North Korea is most responsible for derailing the limited nascent progress. Since the 1960s there has been a long litany of these events: the Pueblo affair, the EC-121 case, the D.M.Z. axe murders, the terrorist attack on the Blue House, the murder of President Park's wife, the digging of invasion tunnels, periodic kidnappings of South Koreans in third countries, the Rangoon bombing, the KAL 007 attack which North Korea tacitly approved, and many lesser known terrorist and espionage incidents. The November 1987 bombing of a Korean Air flight from the Middle East by North Korean agents is the latest of such events. North Korea uses for its pretexts allegations of border provocations, U.S.-R.O.K. preparations for war under the guise of massive field exercises, U.S. offensive nuclear deployments, and U.S. connivance with Japan to reconquer all of Korea. The rationales of the U.S. and South Korea are far more solidly founded than the flimsy excuses of North Korea. However, that is not the point here. Even though the R.O.K. and U.S. may be more justified in making their cases than is North Korea, the key factor is the enthusiasm of all sides for pretexts to stymie talks that they really are not interested in concluding.

Despite much rhetoric from all parties, little has been done to break the stalemate on the Korean peninsula. Fortunately, the U.S. in the 1980s—at long last—contributed to the gradual movement toward improved U.S.-D.P.R.K. relations. Washington first experimented with a slightly more flexible attitude toward North Korea in 1983 by engaging in what Seoul skeptics labeled "smile diplomacy," allowing U.S. diplomats to be less aloof and gratuitously cool toward North Koreans at diplomatic functions. But smile diplomacy was another victim of the North Korean terrorist attack on South Korean leaders in Rangoon. Since then, despite a feeble attempt by North Korea in 1984 to open its economy to the West by adopting a variation of Chinese style economic reforms, Washington has reverted to its former hardline position.

Between Rangoon and early 1988 North Korea has done nothing to warrant an improved American attitude. It is still a heavily armed, pugnacious, obstreperous, and dangerous state that seriously threatens a close U.S. ally, endangers the peace and security of a crucial region of the world, engages in disruptive acts in far-flung parts of the world, and shows signs of helping the Soviet Union bolster its presence in Asia. Washington would be entirely justified in trying to keep North Korea a pariah state. The trouble with this logic is that pursuing an unchanging hardline policy toward North Korea does nothing to ameliorate the causes of North Korean behavior. So, despite understandable emotional impetus to shun North Korea, Washington again shifted its policies toward Pyongyang in early 1987. The U.S. revived smile diplomacy, citing its desires to smooth the way for the Olympic's success and to encourage North and South Korea to resume their dialogue.

Washington took another long overdue step in 1987 by cautiously signaling American willingness to engage in humanitarian and nonstrategic trade with North Korea if Pyongyang—in effect—behaves itself. Good behavior was to be measured by North Korea's handling of the Olympic issue and its willingness to return to the negotiating table. Seoul had real difficulty handling these minor shifts. Its Foreign Minister went to great lengths to describe these real changes as not being truly substantial, not damaging U.S.-R.O.K. relations, and only "a small step forward" in tension-reduction. Though Seoul officially supported the U.S. measures, there were private qualms that caused it to go along with these steps with some reluctance. Seoul hoped the U.S. would not proceed too rapidly in improving its relations with North Korea.

The involvement of North Koreans in the 1987 KAL incident prompted the U.S., in January 1988, partially to reverse its mellower policy by officially declaring North Korea a terrorist state. Washington's move reduced Seoul's doubts about the United States' reliability. The U.S. had little choice in responding adversely to

North Korea's latest terrorism. Washington's reaction was measured and prudent. Nonetheless, it was unfortunate that prospects for improved U.S.-D.P.R.K. relations were derailed again precisely when there appeared to be promise of genuine progress. U.S. relations with North Korea were set back severely, dimming the chances for near-term improvement.

The United States' constrained position regarding its Korean adversary is similar to the situations of the other major powers. Without a major innovative move on the part of one of the powers, it is unlikely any of the others will take the initiative. Therefore, nothing changes. Only the U.S. seems capable of breaking the ice, perhaps because Americans can be most objective and dispassionate about Korean issues since the U.S. is the only concerned state without territorial proximity. Twice, the U.S. seemed on the verge of making a truly innovative move. Unfortunately, both opportunities foundered when Washington's caution collided with harsh North Korean realities. Further exacerbating this stalemate, Washington's perceptions of Korean issues have been heavily filtered by the desires of Seoul and Tokyo for the U.S. to proceed only as far as they suggest. While positive in terms of alliance cohesiveness, Washington's willingness to accept such restraints does not serve direct U.S. interests in tension-reduction. In time, other opportunities will arise for improving U.S.-D.P.R.K. relations which may succeed. On that note, let us turn to a set of recommendations for improving U.S. policy toward Korea.

3 Recommendations for U.S. Policy Toward Korea

United States policy toward Korea is reasonably successful, but there is certainly room for improvement. Americans must carefully evaluate what is sound in current U.S. policy toward Korea and what needs to be improved. The following recommendations touch on a wide array of issues from broad societal ones to relatively narrow functional ones. Some of the issues and recommendations are more pressing than others. Most of the recommendations are predicated on U.S. recognition of South Korea's increased prosperity and military strength. None is intended to lessen the R.O.K.'s value to the U.S. However, a number of them suggest significant changes in U.S.-R.O.K. relations.

Agendas for Programmed Change

U.S. problems with South Korea have been exacerbated, and often left unresolved, because Seoul intentionally drags its bureaucratic feet, or manipulates long term plans to fend off the day of reckoning so long that U.S. officials—to whom promises were made—are either out of office or preoccupied with other matters. Consequently, many problems never get adequately addressed or resolved. To rectify this systemic poison that worsens virtually every outstanding U.S.-Korean problem, a basic procedural recommendation is that the U.S. always implement its policy improvements through an agenda for programmed change that would either 1) fall within one U.S. administration's term in office or 2) would be staffed to guarantee continuity in personnel and an institutional memory deep enough to preclude Korean stalling or obfuscation. If either of these programmed agenda formats are used, any proposed change would stand a better chance of succeeding than it would if pursued in the easily deflected or manipulated manner so common today. Change is inevitable, so why not plan it in a more methodical, coordinated fashion?

The priority ranking of security and economic issues should change. While security remains a crucial U.S. interest in Korea, and concern for it should not be reduced in absolute terms, it has been surpassed by the importance of economic issues. The U.S. should unambiguously view Korea with a new list of priorities: economics, security, politics, and regional affairs. This ranking accords more fully with emerging global U.S. foreign policy objectives. Economic interests no longer derive from security and political issues, but shape them instead. Consequently, Washington's emphasis on economic interests in Korea should be increased in absolute and relative terms, making them the first priority.

The U.S. needs to focus on its economic interests at home and abroad where Americans are dealing with far more prosperous and competitive trade partners and allies. In turn, that focus should inform the ways in which the U.S. pursues its security, political, and regional interests in Korea and elsewhere. This shift in peacetime priorities is, of course, dependent upon the absence of war. Should North-South deterrence collapse, yielding a new round in the Korean War, security should again become the United States' main priority. As with any attempt to establish a priority of U.S. interests, this one, too, must be treated in the real world in specific contexts. On balance, however, the threat of war on the Korean peninsula has moderated sufficiently, and economic tensions have escalated so much, that a new conceptual framework is warranted, placing economic priorities ahead of security priorities. The most opportune time to consider these changes would be after the 1988 Seoul Olympics are over and a new U.S. administration has taken office in 1989. In that regard, the proposals offered here are consciously non-partisan in nature so that any administration might find value in them.

These circumstances have tremendous implications for international relations. Both the United States and the Soviet Union realize that the global struggle for influence has an economic dimension which is as important a criterion of power as military strength. The U.S. once was preeminent on the economic front, with the Soviet Union a poor second. The emergence of Japan, and to a lesser extent West Germany, as strong rivals changed the power hierarchy. During the 1970s and '80s, Japan surpassed the U.S.S.R. on many economic criteria and the U.S. on some. It is now an economic superpower and has the potential for becoming a complete superpower. Japan may never opt for military power again. However, its economic challenge is severe for the U.S. and U.S.S.R., causing both to reemphasize economic recovery and revitalization.

Perestroika may be a Gorbachevian concept unique to the Soviet Union, but a different form of restructuring also is occurring in the U.S. Neither superpower can afford to fail in its economic reconstruction. To do so would jeopardize their claims to strategic preeminence. This development has serious implications for all U.S. allies and trade partners, including South Korea. All must adjust to the changed U.S. priorities. For South Korea, the new American priorities are made more pressing by Korea's proximity to Japan and its very close economic parallels to the Japanese case. For Americans, South Korea is a corollary of the Japanese economic challenge which shapes the post-postwar security environment confronting the U.S. As part of a generic East Asian economic challenge to the U.S. South Korea is now part of the central problem facing the U.S.

Economic Recommendations

The U.S. is faced with significant problems in U.S.-R.O.K. economic relations. The economic issues that divide the U.S. and South Korea are complicated because they are integral to clashing aspects of our respective nationalisms. To examine this, it is necessary to explore the domestic roots of American economic and political frustrations. This is especially important for those, including many Koreans, who seldom pay attention to these concerns.

For all the talk in Seoul and Washington about the compatibility of our two economies, that relationship could exist only in the same uncomfortable ways that the U.S. and Japan are economically compatible. Both the R.O.K. and Japanese economies are based on processing raw materials. Both economies need suppliers of raw materials and consumers of their finished goods. The United States serves as a major supplier and consumer, and—simultaneously—acts as a security benefactor. The U.S. is a very compatible partner from the perspective of its two Northeast Asian allies.

Viewed from the U.S., however, the compatibility match leaves much to be desired in economic terms. Neither South Korea nor Japan have resources to export to the U.S., and neither are anxious to import substantial quantities of U.S. finished goods if they can produce them at home. While the United States' trade relationships with its Northeast Asian allies are large and important, their uneven nature is unsettling for many Americans. Former Senator Eugene McCarthy once correctly described this sort of relationship between the U.S. and a number of its economically advanced trading partners as a perverse new form of colonialism. Many Koreans never see themselves in a "colonial" role versus the U.S., other than as the victim of "economic imperialism." The notion of South Korea being in the colonizing role, along with Japan and Western Europe, is almost inconceivable for Koreans. However, it is a role reversal crucial for the United States' economic future.

Frustrated U.S. Economic Nationalism

This critical aspect of U.S.-R.O.K. economic relations is its Achilles heel. Unless the U.S. learns to live as the supplier of raw materials and consumer of finished goods for an aggregation of foreign "colonialists," and learns to like it, severe problems lie ahead. The latter is true because American economic nationalism will not permit the long term decline or elimination of major sectors of the U.S. economy.

Economic nationalism is a sensitive issue. In theory, the United States' advantages in other aspects of its international economic relations should more than compensate for what appear to be negative factors in a given bilateral relationship. Similarly, the advantages enjoyed by countries like South Korea and Japan in their trade relations with the United States are offset substantially by their vulnerabilities in other economic sectors. Since the United States is the world's largest economy and generally thriving, and both South Korea's relatively small economy and Japan's huge economy are very vulnerable to natural resource disruptions, the theory holds up in practice. This pleases economists and leads many of them in the U.S. and Korea to discount economic nationalism and question the legitimacy of the allegedly "economic" problems between the U.S. and South Korea. They correctly view these uneven relationships as examples of comparative advantage theory at work in the real world.

They are correct in economic terms, but they do not adequately appreciate that the problems of economic nationalism are primarily political because of the ways in which the U.S. has had to compensate in recent years. As the U.S. and Western Europe confronted early low-wage competition from Asia, Americans and Europeans appropriately concluded that it would be foolish to compete by lowering our wages, and opted to become more competitive by increasing the productivity of workers. This was accomplished through improved management, better worker utilization, and automation. As Japan lost its low-wage competitiveness in the face of newly industrializing nation competition, it, too, began to stress high productivity. In time, Japan and West Europe evolved toward a mixture of productivity-based competitiveness and barriers to finished imports that would threaten the production of their own products. The U.S., too, used some of the same means, but it began to shift partially toward lower-wage competition.

The ability of the U.S. economy to create new jobs has been widely praised as evidence of U.S. economic health. While an accurate claim, it does not fully explain the basis of that health. Instead of stressing increased productivity across the board, in large sectors of the U.S. economy American competitiveness was based on a shift toward much lower-paying industrial and service sector jobs. In short, some Americans have compensated for the foreign pressures on the U.S. economy by ratcheting down to labor-intensive, often low-wage, occupations. Instead of competing on our own advanced economy's terms, some Americans are competing on their competitors' less developed terms. In effect, the U.S.

economy operates simultaneously as partly high-tech, ultra-advanced, and very productive, partly sophisticated "colonial" supplier of raw materials, and partly slipping into semi-third world status.

Most U.S. leaders are not perturbed by this, since the U.S. still is the largest economy, and is essentially healthy and vital. Yet, the political implications of any sizeable decline in living standards for a substantial portion of U.S. society are serious indeed. So far, U.S. responses to this situation have been guarded. However, U.S. politicians in both major parties must inevitably meet the demands of a new generation for continued prosperity and the means to attain the "American dream." To cope with this challenge, the U.S. has several ways open to it. It could learn to live with declining expectations, and some Americans counsel learning to adjust to a marked reduction in prosperity and power. However, supine acceptance of this development is not in the American character or tradition. Decline may eventually occur, but it should be fought in every way possible.

Fighting it can be done in one of two ways: outcompeting the rest of the world, or shutting out the rest of the world. Most Americans would prefer the former, because we think we can do it. Free trade remains a popular concept among Americans. They desire free trade in principle and hope to make it work in practice. However, doing so will require the U.S. to demand and receive reciprocal free trade. If that fails, or Americans discover they cannot compete under free and fair trade conditions, the U.S. could opt explicitly to reject free trade in principle and practice. Advocacy of economic self-sufficiency is a very beguiling argument. Intimations of these desires were raised in the 1984 and 1988 U.S. presidential campaigns, but did not become persuasive. If the U.S. becomes frustrated with the inadequacies of the poorly functioning "free trade" system, Americans may yet turn to their own version of what, in the North Korean context, could be called a *juche* model. Obviously, few Americans see much to emulate in the sickly North Korean economic model, but the desire for self-sufficiency and control of one's economic destiny is powerful. Moreover, the U..S. is much more capable of achieving substantial self-sufficiency and control than any of its trading partners.

Without the U.S. advocating such a move, its potential among a nation with deep-seated latent isolationist tendencies should suffice for its foreign trade partners to be more sensitive to American frustrations. These are creating among Americans what Koreans call a sense of *han*, simmering anger that could suddenly boil over. This *han* exists primarily among U.S. elites, but an economic downturn could rapidly expand its influence to the masses. Congressman Richard Gephardt's use of populist criticism of Korean trade practices in his failed 1988 campaign indicated the potential for American *han*'s explosiveness. His willingness to go to retaliatory extremes in order to pry open foreign markets was rejected as too narrow to be "presidential." His message, however, was heeded by all his rivals (in both parties) who committed themselves to fostering free and fair trade conditions that would eliminate American desires to retaliate. Should these efforts fail, and American frustrations intensify, Gephardtist responses remain an American option. In any event, these American frustrations, based on economic nationalism, are likely to become crucial in shaping U.S.-R.O.K. relations.

Candor With Korea

This discussion of background attitudes is intended to demonstrate the highly political nature of the economic issues outstanding between the U.S. and South Korea. In this context some politically tinged steps can be recommended for the U.S. to improve the relationship. The most basic recommendation is that the U.S. be more candid about its own domestic economic problems and recognize the political tensions they cause. South Koreans (and Japanese, Taiwanese, and assorted Europeans) are correct when they argue that the U.S. should shape up its own ability to compete. We Americans must work harder at reforming our economy and learning to penetrate foreign markets. This combination is the basic solution to American economic problems. However, market opening alone is not enough. The U.S. economy must be capable of competing once it gains access to those markets. Moreover, even if total foreign market access were achieved and American exporters

41

were fully successful overseas, exports cannot compensate for domestic economic ill-health. At best, success overseas can reinforce a strong domestic economy. The solution to U.S. economic problems cannot be found overseas or extracted from trade rivals in the form of concessions.

Nonetheless, foreign markets remain important in this context. The U.S. needs to devote more attention and skill to a wide array of potential foreign customers for American products. The smaller South Korean market is not worth the effort of the Japanese market, but it is comparable to some major European markets that Americans do not glibly write off. Hence, Americans should redouble their efforts to penetrate the Korean market, too. However, U.S. export efforts can be irrelevant if foreign markets are not opened enough to give Americans an equal and fair chance. Foreign protectionism also constrains the prospects for U.S. domestic economic health.

Seoul may never be very responsive to U.S. requests for greater opening of the R.O.K. market to American products, if those requests are based primarily on U.S. interests. Needed is a pitch to Seoul which shows that the damage inflicted on portions of the U.S. economy by South Korea, and a flock of other countries with policies similar to Korea's, could threaten the long term vitality of the U.S. as a superpower capable of defending its allies, including South Korea. Hence, what Seoul should be asked to do to help the U.S. economy must be posed in ways that demonstrate that positive Korean responses would directly serve R.O.K. interests.

The United States is not truly accustomed to asking South Korea to help even though we are doing it more often in the late 1980s. Americans have been used to telling Seoul what it expects and South Koreans, in the past, were used to heeding American desires. This relationship is changing rapidly. South Koreans no longer ask, "how high?," when they are told by Americans to jump. The client state behavior of South Koreans is markedly diminished. This is especially true of younger Koreans. Consequently, it is important that Americans learn to treat South Koreans with more respect. The U.S. must treat the R.O.K. like an ally and trade partner which has graduated from the ranks of the client states. Americans must learn how to appeal to South Korean national interests in a more sophisticated way. There must be less emphasis on manipulation of South Korea and less readiness to use crude leverage. Throughout the remainder of these recommendations the terms "leverage" and "influence" are used extensively to describe how Americans should pursue U.S. goals in Korea. In all these cases, it is crucial that Americans approach Korea with respect and try to attain U.S. objectives through the sophisticated use of leverage and influence. This is the best way to appeal to Korean interests in ways that might benefit the United States.

Those interests require some sympathy by Americans in security, economic, and political affairs. The security sympathy Seoul could depend upon from Americans in the past still exists, but is dissolving as South Korea's need for U.S. military support is seen by Americans as an onerous burden, better borne by South Koreans themselves. Similarly, the encouragement Seoul could once routinely expect from the U.S. for South Korean economic growth also still exists, but is eroding by American questioning of the wisdom of fostering allied economic prosperity at the expense of the U.S. economy. The image of South Korean prosperity conveyed by the 1988 Seoul Olympics may underscore such American perceptions. South Korea cannot continue as it is if the U.S. economy is not strong, and the security network based on that economy cannot be relied upon.

South Korea alone can never do enough to relieve the United States' problems. Neither can Japan, nor any other country alone, do enough. At best, perhaps 25% of the United States' trade deficit will be resolved by removal of foreign trade barriers. Elimination of non-tariff barriers would help further, but would not eliminate the U.S. deficit. One recurring nightmare for U.S. trade officials envisions the total elimination of all impediments to American access to foreign markets—followed by American failure to compete in those markets, and no significant improvement in the deficit. It also is necessary to remember that the U.S., for all its free trade rhetoric, retains many trade barriers and subsidies. Nonetheless, having acknowledged these limitations, there is a valid case to be made for increasing American pressures on the United States' trade partners to open their markets on a fair basis.

Market-opening pressures on South Korea, and other Asian countries, must be kept in this perspective and must be part of a broader effort. Aggregated U.S. pressures—based on appeals to collective interests—on a wide range of countries should motivate many or all of the United States' trade challengers to cooperate in some measure. If they do not, they can expect to arouse American anger and retaliation. This is crucial for South Korea, because it is among the most vulnerable of these trading partners to U.S. retaliation. Thus, while Americans should not single out South Korea for harsh criticism or retaliation, unless it can be demonstrated that Seoul is especially to blame, neither should the U.S. single out the R.O.K. for unusually gentle coddling. It should be confronted no more than any other trade partner, but no less either.

Dealing With "Korea, Inc."

The U.S. should be candid about comparing the R.O.K. and Japan, and how these two countries ought to be treated in U.S. policy. South Korean officials, acdemics, and businessmen are adamant that their country is not a "new Japan." Though technically accurate, because of the differences in history, scale, defense burden, and national debt, their arguments fail in terms of each country's economic orientation and impact on the U.S. The notion that "Korea, Inc." does not exist or parallel "Japan, Inc." is nonsense. If anything, that paradigm is more evident in South Korea, and the U.S. should be candid in saying so.

The South Korean version of command- or guided-capitalism is far more centralized and rigidly controlled than Japan's. Government, military, business, and academic interaction is very close in South Korea. Hierarchical societal ties based on age, family, education, provincial background, or other factional criteria are at least as powerful in South Korea as in Japan. In the South Korean business world a few companies are noted for their independence from government. The best example is Samsung. However, most companies—whether *chaebol* (conglomerates) or medium-sized firms—are more inclined to cooperate with government guidelines partly because they are vulnerable to government pressures to conform, but mainly because they trust the advice of government technocrats who enjoy a good track record, who have access to information, and who usually are motivated by ambitions consonant with the national interest. In short, there is a profound hand-in-glove relationship between many of these companies and the government. That is what "Korea, Inc." means and it clearly exists. A few companies are even more tightly wedded to government control, such as Posco (Pohang Iron and Steel Co.), which is a semi-government corporation. However, extreme examples are not needed to prove that "Korea, Inc." is alive and well.

The reason the U.S. should be candid about the existence of the "Korea, Inc." parallel to Japan is simple: it clears the way for the U.S. to treat South Korea the same way it does Japan. Many South Koreans and their American friends fear the prospect of the U.S. lumping the R.O.K. into Japan's category. However, this is both inevitable and desirable. South Korea may not be a "new Japan" yet, but it wants to be. The U.S. has enough trouble with one Japan; it does not need another. Consequently, the U.S. is justified in treating South Korea in a preemptive fashion so that it never poses the challenges to the U.S. that Japan does. Though this proposal is likely to mean a tougher U.S. stance toward South Korea and Japan, if the U.S. can improve its position vis-a-vis the larger Asian economic challenge, this proposal should benefit South Korea, over the long run. If Japan grants fairer U.S. access to the Japanese market, U.S.-Japan economic interdependency is likely to intensify in ways that would also benefit other countries that become part of an extended U.S.-Japan-centered integrated economic system. South Korea could easily be one of those countries.

The suggestion to lump South Korea along with Japan in a preemptive manner does *not* mean that the U.S. should stymie South Korean economic growth or exclude it from U.S. markets. However, the U.S. has every right to ensure that South Korean growth and access to U.S. markets is not excessively at the expense of the U.S. economy, and occurs under conditions of two-way free and fair trade. Americans must understand that Korea, Inc.'s way of doing business is a manipulative approach to economic development and trade. Many South Korean leaders are patriotic economic nationalists and nation-builders whose mercantilist instincts are not compatible with their rhetoric about an interdependent, free trading, and internationalist world order. It is crucial that Americans understand these characteristics of our Korean trade partners and learn to cope with them in an equally "patriotic" manner.

Dealing With Seoul's Tactics

South Korean rhetoric is beguiling, but its concommitant actions almost always lag far behind. Seoul has some justification for this sluggishness because there is a significant dissonance between Seoul's stated intentions and the process of implementation by its bureaucracy. Some of this may be inadvertent, but much of it appears intentional. Seoul appears intent upon applying to economic cooperation policy the foot-dragging tactics so useful in U.S.-R.O.K. security relations. Procrastination, postponements, and prolonged negotiations are calculated to deter or deflect Americans, who often have little patience. All too frequently these tactics bar the resolution of trade frictions as they hindered addressing security frictions. One wonders whether Koreans employing these tactics go home and laugh at the gullibility of Americans who—like Charlie Brown and his periodic bouts with Lucy holding the football— never seem to learn and always return smiling, for more. Americans must learn how Koreans negotiate with, and manipulate, the United States. The U.S. should counter these tactics with clear cut agendas for programmed change that cannot be easily deflected, postponed, altered, or defeated by South Korea, or its American lobbyists, several years into the programmed agenda.

If the U.S. gets tougher and more persistent with South Korea (and other trade partners) in trade negotiations, unambiguously discourages a patron-client relationship, and does not shy away from legitimately lumping South Korea into a broader Japan-focused trade policy, it stands an excellent chance of succeeding. Keeping our policies toward Japan, and "new Japans," artificially discreet is a recipe for defeat. A unified policy, with appropriate appendices for distinct situations would be more effective in correcting a wide range of common political problems. It also would help by necessitating greater coordination within the U.S. Government.

The U.S. is greatly weakened in all trade negotiations by poor coordination between its executive and legislative branches. Several major agencies, other small specialized offices, and their respective watch-dog committees in both houses of Congress, with their diverse staffs, constitute a hodgepodge of decisionmaking channels. For these disparate actors to attempt to produce and implement effective and equitable trade policies for several countries is a guarantee that whatever tentative policies emerge will be derailed sooner or later, achieving little enroute. It is far better to consider broad-based and equitable trade laws, designed to achieve fairness with all of the United States' trade challengers who engage in unfair trade practices. New trade laws cannot be panaceas, but—if well administered—they might help to pry open closed markets overseas, providing American exporters opportunities now denied them. The Reagan administration's January 1988 revocation of duty-free trade privileges for Taiwan, Singapore, Hong Kong, and South Korea was a step in the right direction. In Asia, the prime target of such laws must be Japan. Purposeful spillover to countries like South Korea should be sought and used. There is no need to apologize for this practical and equitable approach.

Influencing Seoul

As part of that broad approach, the U.S. should press hard for sharp cuts in South Korea's formal barriers to U.S. products, an improved dollar/won exchange rate, and—most difficult—a profound change in Korean cultural attitudes toward imports. The U.S. should heed the pragmatic advice given by American business representatives on the scene in Seoul. The American Chamber of Commerce in Korea is a feisty organization which stands up for U.S. economic interests. The AMCHAM report of June 1987, is a devastating critique of the inequalities in U.S.-R.O.K. economic relations. Its sound advice should be read by Americans interested in trade policy and incorporated into U.S. policy by Washington.

AMCHAM cites a number of key problems. The R.O.K. pro-
hibits U.S. companies from importing, warehousing, or distribut-
ing American products in Korea, thus hampering sales efforts. Seoul
insists that such efforts be channeled through Korean intermedi-
aries which it can manipulate. There are outrageous R.O.K. duties
and special taxes that triple the cost of a U.S. car sold in Korea,
while Korean cars sold in the U.S. only face a duty of 2.6%. Congressman Gephardt's presidential campaign rhetoric about "$48,000
Hyundais" was excessive, but not erroneous in principle, as the
AMCHAM report specifies. There is a clear "anti-import bias"
in the R.O.K. Customs Service's administrative practices. This bias
is compounded by Seoul's refusal to publish timely and binding
customs regulations in English and its manipulation of vague Korean
language rules. Though specialized, the R.O.K.'s use of military
sales "offset" programs as a device to transfer technology and jobs
from the U.S. to South Korea has broad impact and aggravates U.S.
frustrations. All of these problems can be resolved by seeking
reciprocal fairness in U.S.-R.O.K. economic relations through a
campaign to influence Seoul to treat American exporters fairly.
American firms seeking to export to South Korea should not have
to face stringent R.O.K. restrictions that their Korean counterparts
exporting to the U.S. do not confront.

As noted earlier, U.S. influence in Seoul is gradually declining.
Hence, in an area of economics so crucial to U.S. well-being, the
U.S. should intensify its use of whatever legal, military, and diplomatic levers remain available. It need not be apologetic about using
them. This does not mean that U.S. officials should overreact by
twisting every Korean arm in sight, or engaging in crude blackmail techniques, which are not credible to Seoul and only exacerbate U.S.-R.O.K. frictions. The U.S. should, however, seek and
use practical leverage now, while it is still usable. The longer the
U.S. waits for R.O.K. concessions on cooperation, the less likely
it is that sophisticated American leverage will work.

Making the need for timely and persistent U.S. pressures on
Seoul's trade policies even more important is the certainty that
American lobbyists working for South Korea will exert every effort
to diminish the declining levels of U.S. influence in Seoul by

attacking American policy initiatives in Korea with countervailing pressures on the U.S. home front. It is, of course, South Korea's right, under the U.S. system, to lobby for its economic (and other) interests. It is a skillful way to pursue South Korean interests. Many countries do it, so there is no special blame attached to South Korea. However, Americans must understand the caliber of R.O.K. lobbying, with some big American guns in its arsenal.

Reagan advisor Michael Deaver gained notoriety for lobbying on Seoul's behalf soon after he left office. In 1986 South Korea ranked second only to Japan in the number of registered foreign agents working on its behalf (39 vs. 87), mainly on economic issues. These included many elite Washington lobbying firms, such as Grey and Co. Additionally a number of prominent ex-U.S. government officials who worked on trade, Asia, or foreign policy are advisors for either the R.O.K. government or South Korean firms.

There is an appropriate response the U.S. can make to undercut Seoul's (and any other country's) lobbying efforts. Without paranoia over the effectiveness of Seoul's American advisors—some only symbolically prestigious names for Korean corporate letterheads—the U.S. should respond in kind. The U.S. government has representatives in Seoul, engaged in lobbying of sorts. However, much more lobbying could be done by the U.S. private sector. American firms—with or without Washington's backing—should engage in a serious lobbying effort in Seoul (and elsewhere in Asia) aimed at breaking down barriers to trade and facilitating cooperation with U.S. trade initiatives. Lobbying could be effective, even though South Korea is not run by competing interest groups as is the United States. There are enough economic, financial, and political levers available to sensitive and aware U.S. lobbyists in Seoul, and a cadre of Korean "hired guns," comparable to those hired by South Koreans in Washington. Lobbying is a useful tool for South Koreans in the U.S. and it could be equally effective for Americans in Korea. Lobbying in Korea must be accorded a much higher priority by Americans.

Know Thy Adversary

To exert pressures on, or lobby in, South Korea, Americans should understand much better the bureaucratic and decision-making styles of the R.O.K. government and South Korean firms. It is impossible to accomplish much in Korea if its culture and operational processes are poorly understood in the U.S. Perhaps the greatest misconception among Americans concerned with Korea involves our perception that its decision-making style is akin to the well-known consensual orientation of the Japanese. Ironically, despite their disavowals of being a "new Japan," South Koreans try to persuade themselves and foreigners about their allegedly happy family, harmonious, and consensus-oriented style of decision-making and management. Koreans who peddle this propaganda would like to believe it themselves and, in a sense, aspire to it because it is good Confucian theory. Also, many Korean firms are family run operations, overseen by the founding father.

However, reality in Korea is entirely different from theory. Both the South Korean governmental and commercial worlds are markedly authoritarian, hierarchial, unegalitarian, and run by well-defined bosses whose word is final. The pretense of harmony is window dressing to make bureaucratic and corporate minions feel better, even as they toe the line. This is not to say that many bosses are uncaring or callous. There is a sense of familial responsibility reinforcing their group-think organizational structures which Koreans bring to the work-place from their group-oriented Confucian cultural heritage. However, that work-place family is dominated by the father figure who—at his best—may be caringly paternalistic, but—at his worst—is tyrannical. In any case, the boss is the boss and scarcely tolerates dissent or factionalism.

It is crucial to bear in mind these factors as Americans devise and implement improved trade policies. When dealing with Korea, the U.S. need not be too concerned about decision-making delays or difficulties in deciphering who is really authorized to make decisions, as the U.S. must in Japan. Koreans sometimes take advantage of American willingness to be circumspect and non-offensive in negotiations with Koreans because of earlier experiences with Japan. While Americans should be polite and sensitive to Korean manners, we can afford to be more direct with Koreans than with Japanese. So, when dealing with real decisionmakers in the South Korean government or corporate world, American advocates of a given policy change should not be deflected by Korean excuses about their need to seek internal consensus. If senior Americans deal only with top Korean decisionmakers, and they should insist on doing so, much more can be accomplished promptly.

To be more effective, the U.S. should consciously adopt a slogan-like label to identify the pressure campaign the U.S. might wage against the Asian trade challengers. The label can be most useful to rally the American popular support necessary to make such a campaign persuasive to the trade partners. Perhaps the best contemporary candidate for that role is the reasonably well-known phrase "fair trade." It is applicable worldwide and implies the necessary expansion of one-way free trade into a two-way, market-opening approach. As important, it is popular among Republicans and Democrats. Any label which is used by politicians ranging from Ronald Reagan to Jesse Jackson—such as "fair trade"—must be nonpartisan. A second, corollary slogan for U.S. fair trade initiatives in Asia, also is worthwhile. They should be labeled part of a new "open door" economic campaign. This phrase has name recognition in Asia and could be of great symbolic use for Americans who seek to open South Korea's (and other Asian countries') doors fully to American competition.

Americans also must be much more persistent. Seoul uniformly insists it is doing everything it can, given its constraints. Americans should not accept those constraints as legitimate obstacles to the South Korean market opening to U.S. products—unless Seoul also is willing to accept the imposition of corresponding U.S. constraints (i.e., forces advocating protectionism and economic independence). Since Seoul cannot, and will not, accept such U.S. "constraints," neither should the U.S. accept R.O.K. constraint arguments that are suspect. Similarly, when Seoul argues that its doors are "opened as much as possible" under such constraints, and Americans are "pushing on an open door," the U.S. must overcome such protestations and diligently work to remove the remaining door stops.

One very useful way to generate interest in U.S.-Korea trade policy is positively linking U.S.-R.O.K. and U.S.-Japan/R.O.K.-Japan trade problems. Assuming that Americans can be candid about the Japan-R.O.K. parallels, as suggested above, there could be great value in positively linking the resolution of U.S. trade difficulties with the R.O.K. to the R.O.K.'s trade problems with Japan. South Korean officials frequently compare the two trade relationships. Americans should stress to South Koreans the heuristic value for the U.S. and R.O.K. of amicably resolving our major trade disputes so that U.S.-R.O.K. economic harmony might be held up as an example by Washington and Seoul for Tokyo's edification. This is important because many Japanese are concerned about competition from South Korea and the prospect that American and South Korean economic cooperation could produce commercial partnerships more capable of competing with Japanese firms. Thus, Americans should be encouraged to see improved U.S.-R.O.K. trade relations as a stepping stone toward an improved U.S. ability to cope with the Japanese challenge.

Washington might consider more seriously than it has, one of the pet notions of many South Korean officials and academics, namely that U.S.-R.O.K. economic cooperation aimed at Japan could benefit commercially both the U.S. and South Korea. There is merit in this idea and it could be used in certain instances, but Americans should not see it as a panacea. The basic flaw in it is that South Koreans, despite easier cultural access to Japan, are only slightly more successful in Japan than Americans because of the widespread Japanese prejudice toward Koreans. It is doubtful that Americans would gain much by being identified with Koreans in the Japanese public's mind. Nevertheless, the idea should be pursued because there are real possibilities for forming cooperative economic ventures that would enhance the capabilities of American and South Korean firms to deal with Japan. Joint U.S.-R.O.K. efforts could make a powerful combination in Japan, each side's strengths supplementing the weaknesses of the other.

Positive Trade-Defense Linkages

If the U.S. tries diligently on several relatively benign fronts without prying the South Korean market open as fully as American businessmen want, more assertive steps might be taken. One, now assiduously avoided by U.S. officials, is overt linkage between U.S. security and trade policy. Avoiding this linkage is a serious mistake. It is, potentially, one of the strongest and most effective levers the U.S. possesses. This linkage has been raised in many other contexts—notably in NATO and Japan—and firmly rejected by U.S. policymakers. There is widespread criticism of efforts to link defense and trade policy on the well known grounds that it would be too easily abused by forces favoring protectionism, might violate international trade agreements, would be difficult to administer in Washington, and would have to be applied universally with uncertain results. Most American foreign policy specialists remain opposed to this approach to linkage for these reasons. The present proposal must be considered in that context.

Those views were appropriate for earlier conditions when the U.S. economic and defense posture could afford to be more magnanimous. Keeping trade and defense policy discrete is a policy luxury the U.S. can no longer afford. Their separation has been, from the outset, an artificial policy because economic well being has always been integral to the preservation of national security. Given the changed circumstances in which the U.S.—as a superpower—now dwells, surrounded by wealthier allies which still rely on the U.S. to underwrite their security, avoiding trade-defense linkage is becoming a unsound policy. It is a very powerful tool which the U.S. should consider using everywhere. If used in a prudent and sophisticated manner, it could undercut protectionists and facilitate free trade, become central to improved international trade agreements, bring a much needed level of coordination to U.S. executive and legislative branch interaction, and infuse greater fairness into U.S. relations with many countries. It is a policy option worth considering seriously, including in U.S. relations with South Korea.

This linkage should not be used in the crude, simplistic manner sometimes suggested by contemporary American critics of U.S. policies toward Korea. This would be foolish in Korea, or anywhere else. There is no U.S.-R.O.K. economic problem so serious that the U.S. would threaten cutting its strategic support if Seoul does not make certain economic concessions. However, there are many circumstances that would warrant a more sophisticated U.S. use of its security leverage. This is the context in which trade-defense linkages should be considered. Because the R.O.K. needs U.S. security support, it cannot afford to weaken the U.S. economy or to arouse American popular antagonism over its trade policy that could spill over into the U.S. commitment to R.O.K. security. Such linkages, if phrased in terms of non-punitive rewards for positive responses to U.S. needs, could be very useful and should be pressed diligently. This approach is entirely different from the crude threat techniques usually associated with proposals for linking trade and defense policy.

A related technique would involve pressing South Korea for trade concessions on econo-strategic grounds that Seoul's security-conscious elites understand better than most of the United States' allies/trade partners. While commercial protectionism is often seen as narrow-minded and greedy by many in the U.S. and R.O.K.—at least in terms of U.S. protectionism—there is another form which might be considered in the U.S.: "strategic protectionism." In essence, it is legitimate for the U.S. to preserve its defense industrial base because it is vital that the U.S. maintain such capabilities. The U.S. already subsidizes and indirectly protects areas of its economy for security purposes.

The sensitive issue is, how far should a country go in protecting its defense industrial base? Koreans, for example, would not mind the U.S. becoming partly or substantially dependent on the R.O.K for a defense-related product such as steel. Moreover, there is nothing intrinsically wrong with such bilateral dependence among allies. On the contrary, it is a valuable aspect of economic interdependence which helps motivate desires for collective security. However, when a wide range of dependent bilateral relationships are aggregated, the U.S. might be overly dependent on the combination. Against this background, Washington could make a legitimate case for ensuring the U.S. economic foundation, which sustains viable collective security. That would permit it to seek the cooperation of a range of allies to change their trade policies that collectively erode the U.S. defense-industrial base. Because of the allies' concerns for U.S. economic well being, and strategic resilience, they should be encouraged to make appropriate concessions that may help the U.S. economy retain sufficient strength. Those arguments are likely to be particularly persuasive to many South Korean leaders who understand thoroughly the need for a broad and resilient economic base to undergird national security.

Exerting Indirect Influence

It also may be possible to improve U.S. economic policy toward Korea through indirect approaches. The U.S. should analyze and consider whether there is anything in the South Korean societal approach to economic issues that might be used by the U.S. to its advantage. There are two significant opportunities to exert indirect influence in South Korean economic affairs. One involves the changing motives behind South Korean economic growth. Originally driven by desires to create a stronger state capable of defending itself, South Korean economic growth increasingly is driven by narrower profit motives. However, there are many South Korean leaders who still prefer a more altruistic ambition. There must be elements within the ambiguity and inhibitions felt by some prominent South Koreans regarding capitalist profit—stemming from traditional Confucian concerns with propriety and disdain for personal aggrandizement—which U.S. policymakers could redirect to fashion a more effective trade policy. American trade negotiators should try to play off those altruistic South Koreans against the more profit oriented among them. The approach might work elsewhere in Confucian Asia as well, but Korea probably would be a good test case because it is so heavily Confucian and is torn by its ethical ambiguity.

The other opportunity is present in the already cited discontinuity between R.O.K. policy reform pronouncements and bureaucratic realities. While recognizing this split's importance for Seoul's foot-dragging style, the U.S. also should see this as an opportunity to use the divisions within Seoul's elites to play one against the other.

These divisions and the differing perspectives between security, political, and economic bureaucracies probably come as close as anything in Seoul to the divisions in Washington which Seoul and its lobbyists do not hesitate to manipulate. In short, the U.S. ought to become much more creative in its attempts to influence these groups in Seoul.

Neither tactic should be construed as an effort to disrupt or undermine the South Korean economy. That economy is important to the U.S. as the motor of a thriving U.S. ally and an integral portion of the global economy. However, Americans have every right to seek and use any levers available to the U.S. in negotiating with South Koreans, or anyone else. After all, South Koreans do not hesitate to take advantage of our societal and bureaucratic divisions for their purposes. There is nothing wrong with Americans doing unto South Koreans what they do unto us. This twist on the golden rule would help create a degree of reciprocal fairness in the bilateral economic relationship.

Security Recommendations

Turning next to U.S.-Korea security relations, how might they be improved? There are steps that should be taken to improve this facet of the relationship that is strained by changes in the economic stature of the U.S. and its Northeast Asian allies. None of the following recommendations are offered in a negatively critical manner. The defense arrangements between the U.S. and South Korea certainly work. They accomplish their mission. However, as one pundit said, "Good enough, never is!" In short, simply because a system functions reasonably well does not mean that it should never be tinkered with, overhauled—even tossed out—if something better is possible.

Some periodic minor adjustments made in U.S.-R.O.K. defense relations are precisely that. They amount to a reshuffling of chairs, putting a rearranged facade on the same basics. Small changes need not all be cosmetic, of course. Incremental upgrades in armaments and tactical skills are often made by officials on both sides of the relationship. Many are worthwhile and improvements of that sort need encouragement. This is the programmed change the bureaucracy does best and it should be given due credit. However, asking bureaucrats to rethink the fundamental reasons for their institutional existence is rarely productive. This is graphically demonstrated in the reactions elicited from both sides when asked to review the prospects for major changes in U.S. strategy in support of the R.O.K. Though there is a low-key routine debate over the pros and cons of current U.S. strategic objectives in Korea, so far no significant changes have occurred. Here, too, however, defense planners on both sides should be given credit for contemplating the prospects for long term changes in areas such as command relationships. Slowly but surely both sides are getting ready for future changes though they seem uncertain about what changes are likely.

Keeping U.S. Forces In Korea?

Jimmy Carter was neither the first American nor will he be the last to ask why American forces are still in Korea so long after Korean War hostilities supposedly abated since the 1953 truce. Part of the standard answer to this query—which will be asked as long as U.S. forces remain in Korea—is implicit in the wording of the previous sentence. The war never actually ended, so the rationale for U.S. forces never ended either. Of course, that rationale has been changed and reinforced by the growth of the R.O.K.'s economy and strategic value. There are valid reasons for U.S. forces to be in Korea, but those reasons have changed enough to warrant a basic rethinking of their best roles in Korea, how long they should stay there, and how they should interact with R.O.K. forces.

The most common reason for wanting them out is a straightforward one—they do not need to be there because South Koreans can do the job for themselves. That sentiment lay behind Carter's proposal. The logic of that argument is persuasive. It is true that South Koreans are far more capable of defending themselves now than they were in 1950, '60, '70, or '80. The R.O.K.'s armed forces in 1988 are nearly capable of doing the whole task themselves. Most American defense analysts believe that—except for air, naval, and "strategic" forces—South Korea can defend itself. However, those are major exceptions. The R.O.K. also has a legitimate need for certain categories of U.S. ground and logistical support, but that support no longer requires that the U.S. maintain the spectrum of forces it now has in Korea. The U.S. should consider invoking the implicit "sunset clause" in its security treaty regarding the military need for American ground forces in Korea to protect against North Korean aggression. The rationale for keeping U.S. ground forces in South Korea is much weaker today than it was a decade or two ago.

That being so, one might expect renewed calls from Americans to pull U.S. forces out of Korea in the coming years. Some of these will come from neo-isolationist elements seeking an overall U.S. retrenchment. A relevant example was The CATO Institute's "Korea: The Case for Disengagement." Rebutting these calls may be difficult, but necessary for reasons cited below. Others will argue on grounds staked out by conservative scholar Melvyn Krauss, of the Hoover Institution, who argues that withdrawing U.S. troops from N.A.T.O. is necessary to jolt Europeans toward self-reliance. Krauss extended that theory to the Korean context by advocating the withdrawal of U.S. troops from South Korea to avoid interference in Seoul's affairs, allow South Korean self-reliant nationalism to flourish, and—interestingly—because "A troop pullout, by raising the specter of a more militaristic South Korea, will force Japan to modify its minimalist defense posture." This would, of course, be in line with U.S. pressures on Japan to be more self-reliant. Still others argue that U.S. forces should be pulled out, or severely cut back, because their presence reinforces the same Korean militarism which Krauss wants to use as leverage. All these arguments have some validity, but neither alone nor collectively are they of enough merit to warrant a pullout of U.S. forces any time soon.

What should the U.S. do, then? Hunker down for an indefinite stay, for as long as Seoul wants American forces to stay? A minority of conservative Americans who are very close to South Korean leaders, viewing the situation on the peninsula from a security perspective favoring South Korea rather than one serving U.S. national interests, seems prepared to yield the decisions to Koreans. In essence, they say the U.S. should keep its forces in South Korea as long as Seoul needs them. Such views are frequently expressed at policy-oriented academic conferences on U.S.-Korean relations. Such attitudes are unwarranted and should not influence U.S. policy. This is not to suggest that U.S. policy should be made without consulting Seoul, but the decisions are legitimate only if they serve U.S. interests. American forces must not be in Korea for one day after the moment when their presence is not demanded by U.S. interests. We should take note of a comment made by Rep. Lee H. Hamilton (D., Indiana), Chairman of the Europe and Middle East subcommittee of the House Committee on Foreign Affairs, who said of the U.S. commitment to N.A.T.O. in mid-1987, "Congress is not demanding that the troops come home; it is merely inquiring why they must continue to stay?"

A review of the U.S. force presence in Korea also is long overdue and should be conducted by executive branch agencies in consultation with the congress. Many conservatives in the U.S. and South Korea would reject that move as too risky because it could loose political forces that might wreak havoc with U.S. strategy toward Korea. North Korea might well misinterpret U.S. motives in engaging overtly in a policy review or holding legislative hearings. Furthermore, such Korea hearings could become a gratuitous platform for zealots. These concerns should not be feared. If balanced and carefully explained policy reviews and hearings are held to discern whether the U.S. should keep its armed forces deployed in Korea, the analysis would show that it is very much in the United States' interests to keep our forces there.

Defining Vital Interests

Any hearings must candidly address the definition of "vital" U.S. interests in Korean security. If one defines "vital" as determining the survival of a country, the only state with truly vital interests at stake in the defense of South Korea is the R.O.K. Its existence is at risk. In contrast, should the worst occur, and South Korea go the way of South Vietnam, the U.S. would survive. To be sure, the U.S. would feel the loss of a close ally, valued trade partner, key buffer in the defense of Japan, American credibility, and—last but certainly not least—many friends. However, it would be far from a fatal blow to the U.S. and many Americans would soon put such a setback out of their minds almost as quickly as they have dismissed the Republic of Vietnam from their consciousness. South Korea's intrinsic importance and proximity to Japan make it more valuable to the U.S. than South Vietnam ever was, but Americans would not be devastated by the loss of the R.O.K. Consequently, routine American characterization of U.S. interests in Korea as "vital" is not credible. This may seem a harsh judgment, but candor in these matters is essential.

The R.O.K. has vital interests in the security commitments it enjoys from the U.S. The reverse is not yet true and may never be true. That is not to suggest that U.S. security interests in Korea are unimportant. South Korea is a valued ally and trade partner. More important, its geopolitical value imbues it with regionally vital qualities. Secretary Weinberger's approach to American "vital interests" in Korea predicated on a *regional* stake, cited in the key issues section, should become the standard U.S. interpretation.

Security: Altering Roles

Another finding would be certain: though the U.S.-R.O.K. Security Treaty remains valuable, U.S. ground forces are no longer needed to perform the military duties they now fulfill. Their role is essentially political. Soldiers in the U.S. Second Infantry Division deployed near the Demilitarized Zone (D.M.Z.), the main U.S. ground component deployed in Korea, know precisely their function. They are there to fight if they can, to give Seoul—to their south—a bit more time to rally its forces for a counterattack. However, this does not come close to the whole truth. There are Korean soldiers serving on either side of the "2nd I.D." troops, who can fight as well as the Americans, possibly better. Actually, nearly all the front line positions along the D.M.Z. are manned by R.O.K. forces which are well trained, equipped, and confident of their ability to fight better than Americans.

Why then are the Americans sitting squarely in the middle of an invasion route it is assumed North Korean aggressors would likely use? Americans are there because a North Korean invasion is certain to kill large numbers of them in the first stage of the war. Some in the division, with morbid humor, refer to this as their "D.I.P." function, that is, "Die In Place." Political scientists and government officials (none of whom are stationed on the Korean frontline) euphemize this role by referring to it clinically as the "tripwire" role of U.S. forces. This is a decidedly political function. American forces are emplaced in exposed positions so their early involvement in the next Korean War will guarantee an almost automatic decision by the U.S. Congress to let the executive branch keep past promises and come to South Korea's rescue once again. Seoul wants to retain the tripwire because South Korean leaders do not trust Americans to keep their word, meet treaty obligations, and sustain the R.O.K.

This is an enigmatic and arcane situation, made sadder by the years-long complicity in this arrangement by U.S. executive branch officials in several administrations, who also mistrusted the Congress and the American public to be steadfast should North Korea renew the war. Still more wrenching is the probability that those apprehensions were warranted during the Vietnam era, and its immediate wake. Even today, under the tripwire constraints and a supportive U.S. administration, it is not absolutely certain the Congress and public would support all the oral reassurances Washington has made to Seoul for years. In an atmosphere of such persistant doubt one can understand why R.O.K. and American officials might see this de facto blackmail as necessary. However, such views are shortsighted. The U.S. commitment to Korea can be guaranteed more effectively in other ways that do not require U.S. ground forces as presently deployed.

An Improved Tripwire

Beset for years by demands to get U.S. forces out of Korea, nearly all R.O.K. and U.S. officials working on Korean security instinctively reach for their data on the North Korean threat to prove that the U.S. should not pull out. Their perceptions of the North Korean threat are generally accurate. It is very real. North Korean forces are large, well-armed, forward deployed, and ready to attack if directed. If North Korea believed South Korea was greatly weakened, the U.S. irresolute in its commitment to the R.O.K., and substantial support would be forthcoming from China and the Soviet Union, there is no doubt the Kim regime would seize the moment. Though this combination is extremely unlikely, it is possible. The consequences of North Korean success in such a gamble would be disastrous for South Korea, Japan, and the United States. Americans have ample interest in staying in Korea to help the R.O.K. deter that remote prospect. However, the U.S. need not contribute to deterrence in all the ways it does. Keeping U.S. ground forces in Korea, performing their present roles, is a waste of valuable military manpower. There are better ways to use scarce U.S. defense resources, in an age of budgetary constraints, than tying down an entire U.S. Army division in a relatively static function that primarily serves political purposes.

As long as the U.S.-R.O.K. security relationship has a tripwire, to encourage Americans to understand their national interests in Korean security, it need not be the present design. There are better Korean tripwires available to U.S. strategists which would allow the U.S. to use its forces in a more flexible manner. An improved tripwire could be the same 2nd I.D. redeployed, with a modified mission, elsewhere in Korea. Do Seoul officials think Americans so fickle that the U.S. Congress would not permit a U.S. infantry division deployed in the middle of the R.O.K., with a mission to reinforce R.O.K. divisions, to perform that mission in the heat of war? At a minimum, that limited redeployment should be carried out. It would be a show of great U.S. confidence in the R.O.K. and, of course, South Korean self-confidence. It would also render the U.S. military presence in South Korea far less visible to most South Koreans, a real benefit for U.S.-R.O.K. political relations. However, the U.S. should not aim at such half measures because it would still be a profound waste of the division manpower. If the U.S. commitment to the R.O.K. can be guaranteed by a very different deployment, and it can, the U.S. should strive for a programmed phase-out of ground deployments that now characterize U.S. troop placements.

A fair question from skeptics is, "what else can we do for Korea to make the U.S. commitment to the R.O.K. more credible?" The answer requires substituting *"in* Korea" for *"for* Korea." What we now do there is excessively "for Korea" and not enough "for the U.S. in Korea." Perversely, the U.S. commitment to Korean security could be greatly strengthened by making it less focused on Korean security. That, too, may seem contradictory, but it is not. The U.S. suggests that much of what it does in Korea strategically is for the benefit of South Korea. Though partially true, that is also misleading. The U.S. is in Korea militarily for the same reasons it has always had: to protect the U.S. and its regional interests against Soviet encroachment. Because the North Korean threat is part of the larger communist threat, it is only slightly illogical for Americans to argue that what we are doing for South Korean defenses against the northern threat is part of a larger picture. Much less logical has been the insistence of U.S. authorities that American forces were in Korea only to help the R.O.K. against the North. This rings as hollow today as it has for years.

A Regional Rationale

It is time the U.S. adjust its forces in Korea to a more regionally focused role in which burdens would be more equitably shared with South Korea. The rationale for such a role is a global one. In many of its alliance relationships the U.S. now confronts allies who are capable of doing far more for themselves than they do. Despite South Korea's relatively good record as a responsible defense partner, compared to several NATO countries and Japan, it nonetheless enjoys a substantial U.S. strategic subsidy. If the U.S. were to pull its forces out of Korea, Seoul would face enormous increases in its security costs. Retention of U.S. forces enables South Korea to use the defense funds it avoids spending for other purposes, including enhancing its ability to compete economically. When South Korea was a poor developing country these arangements made more sense, but—now that it is one of the East Asian group challenging the U.S. economically—it no longer does.

Consequently, it makes eminent economic and strategic sense for the U.S. to share the burdens of common security with all allies who are capable of upholding a fairer share of such burdens. Many post-World War Two commitments by the U.S. to allies were supposed to protect allies until they could protect themselves. Implicit in these arrangements was a defacto "sunset clause." A long-term U.S. objective in these alliances was to work itself out of the job of providing security for allies. When they were capable of taking care of themselves, they were supposed to do so. South Korea is such an ally and should be pressed to undertake a fairer distribution of military roles. The U.S. and R.O.K. can do much more to pool our military resources, do what each does best, share power, and foster more equitable and interdependent security arrangements.

This is not a simple proposition, considering the historical legacy of the bilateral security relationship. It is not in keeping with past U.S. policy of trying to exclude Korea from superpower tensions. The latter policy long has been artificial because both Korean states have displayed client-state behavior, acting at times as proxies for their superpower backer. Moreover, today, the United States' desire to exclude Korea has been overtaken by events. The Soviet Union and the U.S. already have involved Korea in superpower tensions by making security arrangements with each Korea. Most important, those arrangements have become more explicit on the U.S.S.R.-D.P.R.K. side in recent years. Soviet-North Korean defense cooperation appears to have a distinct regional rationale. It is time the U.S. adjust its formal security arrangements with South Korea to the new circumstances. This adjustment is increasingly feasible because of South Korea's growing economic capabilities. When the U.S. obtained South Korean military assistance for South Vietnam, Washington was accused of using R.O.K. forces as proxies and Seoul was accused of letting its forces become mercenaries for American "imperialism." The proposals made here differ significantly from past R.O.K. cooperation with U.S. strategy because South Korea no longer can be considered a client state and should be treated as a security partner.

Further complicating the proposal, Americans are prone to excessive superpower hubris and overconfidence in our national power. Conversely, South Koreans are prone to an insecurity complex, feeling helpless and vulnerable. Actually, South Koreans are stronger than they think and the U.S. is traumatically adjusting to its relative decline as a power. The U.S. is the superpower core of the Western alliance system, but it is a core which increasingly requires shoring up from all its allies, including South Korea. Fortunately, recognition of this need is gradually growing in the U.S. and among its allies. That is true of South Korean defense planners and intellectuals who sympathize with the U.S. Many of them strive for enhanced cooperation with the U.S. as soon as South Korea is capable of assuming most of the responsibility for its own national defense.

The U.S. ground, air, and naval presence in Korea should be restructured. Those forces should be given a dual function; to respond to a North Korean action, and also to conduct major missions against the United States' superpower adversary which has conducted a major force buildup in the region. U.S. air and naval forces can most easily assume a dual role. Some U.S. ground forces in Korea also should be reconfigured into more mobile deployments to serve these larger, dual, purposes. Eventually, all U.S. ground combat forces in Korea could assume such dual missions, but—in the interim—a portion of U.S. ground combat forces might be left in their current tripwire deployments. By placing the 2nd Division, other Army infantry units, or Marine Corps units, well behind the D.M.Z., they would simultaneously be available for use in another Korean war or—in more likely scenarios—in other potential conflict zones in Asia. In time, as South Korean defense self-reliance and economic conditions permit, South Korean forces will be able to cooperate in regional security. A number of South Korean defense intellectuals now speculate about such future cooperation and seem interested in South Korea performing such roles. The potential missions of U.S. and—some day—South Korean forces throughout the region could include Korean defense, defense of other U.S. allies in Asia (Japan, the Philippines, and others in the Pacific), and forward deployed offensive missions against Soviet installations.

Such missions would, in the aggregate, make the U.S. armed forces in Korea far more important to U.S. national security. Their different tripwire function—though lacking a D.I.P. role against North Korea—would dwarf the value of present static tripwire arrangements. The U.S. would need to defend South Korea to protect these proposed bases that would have unambiguously vital regional roles. The deployment of U.S. forces in that capacity should remain part of U.S. policy so long as the Soviet Union, and its North Korean ally, pose threats to the U.S. and its allies in the region. Should that threat ever dissipate, or our allies become capable of coping with it unilaterally, the U.S. could reconsider its options and probably withdraw all its forces. In the long run, that should remain the United States' goal.

In this light, the proposed shift is not intended as an anti-Soviet move or a way to lock South Korea into an anti-Soviet pact. Its primary purpose is to make the best use of U.S. and R.O.K. forces in Korea. American forces and a subset of South Korean forces can make a much greater contribution to regional security if they are deployed in a more flexible, mobile, and realistic manner. Though one potential mission for these forces would focus on the Soviet Union, there would be many others. Consequently, it would be wrong to interpret the proposed shift as a narrowly anti-Soviet measure. Furthermore, the U.S. and South Korea should be prepared to adjust to credible confidence building measures proffered by the Soviet Union and North Korea. The proposed reconfiguration of U.S. forces in Korea would be no more threatening to U.S. adversaries than are other U.S. forces with flexible missions.

Consequently, it would be wrong to consider these proposed regional bases any more permanent or sinister than are present U.S. installations helping to defend South Korea against North Korean aggression. If the U.S.S.R.'s improved image under Gorbachev is followed by comparable improvements in Soviet foreign and defense policy, the need for U.S.-R.O.K. regional security cooperation would be reduced accordingly. Similarly, improvements in North Korean external policies would reduce the need for U.S.-R.O.K. security cooperation against the North Korean threat. One can only hope—along with many South Koreans—that the 1988 Seoul Olympics will accelerate such developments. Having said that, the time for a total U.S. withdrawal from South Korea, because of lessened tensions, seems distant. Consequently, there is no reason for Seoul to fret over the weakening of the proposed dual-focused tripwire. It is, therefore, feasible for the R.O.K. to move toward manning all its immediate ground defenses, allowing the U.S. to redeploy most of its ground forces. The U.S. should make this one of our goals. A transfer of this magnitude cannot be carried out overnight. Neither, however, need it be prolonged. Seoul should not postpone endlessly, or procrastinate over, such a move. South Korean ground forces are essentially ready to assume the bulk of U.S. ground force roles today. Some R.O.K. and U.S. officers will, however, argue that more time is needed to upgrade R.O.K. capabilities. Because they are specialists in such matters, their views cannot be cavalierly overridden. However, U.S. non-military policymakers should initiate a programmed agenda to complete this transition. It can be done by pinning the U.S. and R.O.K. armed forces to a timetable with specific deadlines for phasing out frontline U.S. ground forces, and phasing in R.O.K. ground forces to replace them.

The only role in this defensive realm that R.O.K. forces may not for a number of years perform as well as U.S. forces, is the intelligence function. Because other types of U.S. forces have legitimate roles to play in Korean and regional defense, the need for U.S. intelligence capabilities in Korea ought to be obvious. Hence, U.S. combat forces deployed in South Korean rear areas could still provide the crucial intelligence to their R.O.K. counterparts when South Korean ground forces replace forward deployed U.S. ground forces near the D.M.Z.

Timetable For A Strategic Shift

How much time should this role assumption by R.O.K. forces and restructuring of U.S. roles require? Once the decision to initiate that policy has been made, the redeployment of U.S. ground forces and substitution of R.O.K. ground forces should not take more than a couple of years to plan and implement. If Seoul agreed in principle, but then started talking about carrying it out over a five-year period, Americans should get nervous and alarm bells sound in Washington. South Koreans are fond of saying, "give us five more years" to carry out some plan or another because they know that within those five years the U.S. administration might well change, a new congressional balance could change pressure for reform, they could get their lobbyists into action, and U.S. bureaucratic allies could sabotage the initiative. Thus, while U.S. reforms should not be precipitous, neither should they be so loosely structured that they can be deflected or aborted by Koreans. The restructuring improvements in R.O.K.-U.S. roles recommended here can, and should, be carried out well within one U.S. administration's term in office.

The shift suggested here toward a more regional focus in the U.S. strategy toward Korea, retaining flexible dual functions, might take longer, but not necessarily. The shift would have to be integrated into the larger U.S. strategy for the Pacific, which could be a slower process. However, the burgeoning Soviet presence in the Pacific, U.S. concerns about improving regional collective security, and—especially—U.S. pressures on Japan to pick up larger defense burdens, render such a shift toward U.S. strategic roles from bases in Korea entirely compatible with larger priorities.

As the post-Reykjavik and post-INF Treaty fears of Western Europeans about new dangers of conventionally armed weakness and U.S. strategic "decoupling" spread to Asia, the U.S. will have added incentives to reinforce its commitment to regional security versus the Soviet Union. This can occur at the same time as it seeks, from a position of strength, to reduce tensions with the Soviet Union. Then, a shift in U.S. roles in Korea would mesh nicely with the global objectives of the U.S. and its Asian allies, emphasizing use of mobile rapid deployment forces and coping with low-intensity conflict scenarios within the region. Such roles cannot be assumed as speedily as a R.O.K. replacement of current U.S. ground force deployments could be effected. There should be more extensive planning and complicated implementation in any U.S. restructuring of its forces in Korea. However, this should not cause problems in overall U.S.-R.O.K. security relations or delay substituting R.O.K. ground forces for U.S. forces.

Once the U.S. commits itself to restructuring its forces in Korea for a dual role, Seoul must have confidence that the U.S. is planning to stay in Korea and protect it, the site of important U.S. bases. Though the timetable for this restructuring might be considerably longer than the relatively short agenda for R.O.K.-U.S. ground force substitution, this should not cause Seoul concern. Once Washington commits itself to a substantial programmatic shift that would strengthen its support for the R.O.K., changes in U.S. administrations, the Congress, or the bureaucracy cannot easily change courses again.

Politically, however, Seoul initially might have problems explaining expanded U.S. and R.O.K. roles to the South Korean people, and certainly could expect to receive added criticism from North Korea. These should not be insurmountable because the partially altered U.S. role and supportive R.O.K. role would symbolize important changes in South Korea's stature. The issue of U.S. forces in Korea constituting a symbol of South Korea's alleged subjugation by Americans would be greatly mitigated—perhaps eliminated—if R.O.K. forces were to play a more equal military role. South Korea would function as an ally more comparable to the British or West Germans, welcoming U.S. assistance but providing substantial help in exchange. This transformation could undercut the arguments of domestic South Korean critics and North Korea. As important, any problems in persuading critics of the shift ought to be more than compensated for by the greater assurances of a durable U.S. commitment and the symbolism of South Korean strategic self-confidence.

Regionalism And Strategic Controversy

Raising this alternative view of Korea's importance to U.S. security, and proposing the shifts recommended above, is controversial. One need only recall the uproar in Seoul caused in 1983 by U.P.I.'s leak of a classified U.S. Defense Department contingency plan that discussed the possibility of the U.S. attacking North Korea or Northeast Asian Soviet facilities in reaction to hostilities in the Middle East. South Koreans have been agitated by similar scenarios scheduled under the rubric of "horizontal escalation" and in the take-the-battle-to-the-enemy precepts of former U.S. Navy Secretary Lehman's "Maritime strategy."

South Koreans, leaders and general public, would prefer to see the U.S. stay in Korea, performing much the same roles it has played there for nearly forty years. If Seoul ultimately insists upon that, it will likely mean an end of that sort of commitment. South Korea can fulfill many of its own self-defense tasks now; if pushed, it could assume nearly all of them very quickly. If the U.S. pulled out, the R.O.K. could rapidly sustain its own self-defense. However, that is not desirable from either the vantage point of U.S. national interests in regional security or R.O.K. national security interests. Seoul should not be afraid of the U.S. postulating regionally or globally important interests that would make U.S. bases in Korea crucial. These proposed shifts would be compatible with R.O.K. national interests. Instead, it should welcome that shift and do everything in its power to cooperate with its U.S. ally to preserve regional peace and security.

The R.O.K. has stressed, almost exclusively, its need for more U.S. help to strengthen R.O.K. forces. That emphasis is understandable because Seoul would like help from the U.S. while conditions are propitious. To use a colloquialism, Seoul's policy is to "get while the gettin's good." It is, in effect, seeking cooperation from the Reagan administration to hedge against the day when a less well disposed administration is ensconced in the White House. Admittedly, South Korea has benefitted from this prudent approach. It could benefit much more if it acted more confidently about its own defenses, encouraged the U.S. to play a leading regional security role that would simultaneously serve U.S. and R.O.K. interests, and did all it could to assist the U.S. and its Asian allies in preserving regional security. Former President Chun almost accepted that concept when, in April 1987, he urged the U.S. to help the R.O.K. bolster its defenses so that South Korea could then help the U.S. by sharing regional security responsbilities. This is a very positive attitude, but Seoul must recognize that R.O.K. economic successes make it capable of greater self-reliance in defense preparedness. If South Korea is to receive further help in upgrading its forces, some of that help ought to come from the United States' other Northeast Asian ally—Japan.

Korean Security: The Japan Factor

Japan's proper role in Korean security is an exceptionally emotional issue. It must be emphasized that this aspect of regional cooperation—while crucial for larger U.S. security interests in Northeast Asia—is not, and should not be interpreted as, a precondition for the proposed shift in the United States' Korean strategy toward regionalism. Ideally, these issues can be linked because the U.S. has similar reasons for pursuing burdensharing and powersharing with each Northeast Asian ally. However, explicit linkage is not necessary for the U.S. to proceed with a regional focus in its security policy toward Korea.

The U.S. has encountered many problems in its security relations with Japan that bear directly on regional defenses important to South Korea. Most U.S. officials concerned with Northeast Asian security assert that Washington now successfully handles these problems. Despite their confidence, assured U.S. access to its bases in Japan for use, in case of another Korean War, remains a delicate issue, only tenuously resolved. American officials are confident that their arrangements with Japan will suffice. The Japanese government seems steadfast in its support of U.S.-R.O.K. security interests. Japanese officials are sympathetic to U.S. and South Korean desires. On the other hand, the Japanese public's understanding of—and support for—the role of the bases, in the event of another Korean War, is very uncertain. Precisely because U.S.-Japanese arrangements for U.S. use of bases in Japan to defend South Korea are not rooted in any popular consensus those arrangements could easily be shaken by a new war in Korea that endangers Japan.

This level of uncertainty underlines the distinct threat perceptions of each ally. Potential Japanese cooperation with the U.S. against the U.S.S.R., if Japanese territory remains inviolate during a U.S.-U.S.S.R. conflict, remains unresolved in terms of popular Japanese consensus to support the United States. Officials of each country remain confident that cooperation will prevail, but American assumptions that the Japanese people will sanction their government's cooperation with the U.S. against the U.S.S.R. rest on shaky premises. Perhaps most important now, U.S. pressures on Japan to upgrade its defenses and to uphold a narrowly defined offshore defense zone—the 1000 mile S.L.O.C. issue—have not progressed as far as persistent U.S. critics of Japan's sluggish security policies would prefer. Consequently, tensions over defense linger despite the efforts of the Nakasone and Takeshita administrations to do more. They flared up in a visible way over Japan's reluctance to assist the U.S. militarily in the Persian Gulf during 1987–88. Japan's refusal to help militarily rankled many American politicians who wondered aloud why the U.S. should protect Japan's oil supply when the Japanese would not cooperate. Perhaps most important over the longer run, U.S.-Japan economic frictions—with their major spillover implications for U.S.-R.O.K. economic tensions—may well have a negative impact on U.S.-Japan security relations. Cumulatively, these U.S.-Japan problems carry tremendous implications for regional security focusing on Korea.

Though it always has been unpopular with R.O.K. officials to point this out, the importance of U.S.-Japan relations long has dwarfed the importance of U.S.-R.O.K. relations. Nascent U.S.-P.R.C. security ties also overshadow U.S.-R.O.K. relations. Seoul's protests about the growing importance of bilateral U.S.-R.O.K. ties notwithstanding, U.S.-Japan ties still tower over them. Seoul's ambiguity about U.S.-P.R.C. ties also looms on the horizon. The U.S.-Japan connection is, as Ambassador Mansfield frequently reminds us, the single most important U.S. external relationship today. It, in turn, is the context in which U.S. interests in Northeast Asia have become vital.

South Koreans may prefer to think that U.S.-R.O.K. relations would be much easier if Japan were not a major power. Nothing could be further from the truth, because if Korea had not been in Japan's frontyard the U.S. is unlikely to have assigned Korea the importance it has. Admitting this does not denigrate South

Korea. Strong U.S.-Japan relations do not displace strong U.S.-R.O.K. relations for they are complementary. However, the priority for the U.S. is almost certain to remain Japan. Both Americans and South Koreans should be more candid about this axiom and work for a stronger trilateral relationship. In the future comparable ties with China may also be feasible. These tasks may not be easy for either the U.S. or R.O.K., but they are necessary and should be encouraged.

Inducing Northeast Asian Trilateralism

The U.S. has been very cautious in dealing separately with its two Northeast Asian allies. It would not be wise for the U.S. to stop being careful and rush headlong into a reckless policy of trying to force Japan and South Korea into instant cooperation. Washington has studiously avoided advocating a more closely linked regional security role for Japan and the R.O.K. that might deepen their antagonism. Japan should never be made to appear as a surrogate for the U.S. The reasons are obvious. Many Asians do not relish seeing Japan play a larger role in the region for any reason. Similarly, many Americans are strongly opposed to this. However, the U.S. has for too long played Japan's surrogate in the region. It is important that Americans and Asians understand why this version of surrogacy is inequitable.

Policy changes in this area will not come easily, but they should be pursued. How long should the U.S. continue to provide Japan's territorial security backstop, its regional security, and its sea lane security in a global context? Americans have every right to complain about persistent Japanese strategic parsimony and self-centeredness. They have every right to examine the linkages between Japan's so-called "free rider" syndrome and its economic successes. Actually, the "free rider" notion is a gross overstatement, but Japan is a "cheap rider." While Japan contributes substantially to the cost of maintaining U.S. forces in Japan and is valued as a technological partner, it does not bear a fair share of the security costs or risks in defense of common interests. In addition, Americans should consider the economic advantages a U.S. defense subsidy provides for Japan to compete with the U.S. It is time the U.S. advocate larger Japanese regional economic, political, and military roles, and urge Japanese cooperation with the U.S. in helping other Asian states (including South Korea) contribute to regional security. There is a need for a joint approach to strategy by Washington and Tokyo, in consultation with Seoul. Americans need not, and should not, apologize to Korea or any other nation for urging such a Japanese role which is emphatically not that of a surrogate for the United States.

Most pointedly, the U.S. should not act as a buffer between Japan and South Korea in strategic affairs. A military alliance may never materialize, though a strong case can be made for one, but there is ample reason for the U.S. to press Japan and South Korea to be more cooperative in an open alignment. U.S. pressure should not be coercive or impatient. Instead, the U.S., together with the R.O.K. and Japan, should create a group of "wisemen" charged with exploring the ways in which trilateral security cooperation might be facilitated. Many officials assert that the private, informal consultations of this nature that already occur are adequate. While such groups are a welcome improvement, they are unable to generate the degree of popular consensus in support of trilateral cooperation necessary for that interaction to be able to withstand pressures from a future crisis. The political controversy which public discussion of enhanced cooperation probably would arouse also would give the eventual agreement firmer popular support.

The most promising basis for such prospective trilateral security cooperation might be adoption by the U.S. and the R.O.K. of Japan's broad-based doctrine of comprehensive security which meshes concerns for economic, political, and military stability. This low-key, inoffensive, and pragmatic approach to security should be—if treated equitably—a viable framework for trilateral cooperation, persuasive to all three nations. South Korea's national interests, in particular, are increasingly compatible with those Japanese national interests which produced the comprehensive security doctrine.

As a buffer, the U.S. lessens the incentives for its two allies to cooperate with each other. So, instead of being anxious to help the R.O.K. or Japan when either seeks U.S. defense assistance, Washington ought to be more open about U.S. desires to first ask whether the assistance sought can be provided by one of the two U.S. allies to the other. Japan has the capabilities and could offer South Korea financial, technological, intelligence, planning, operational exercise, and offshore air and naval assistance. All of these are relatively invisible to the public. Only ground force assistance would seem to be off limits, because of the symbolism of Japanese troops on Korean soil, but South Korea is not likely to need that help because it has ample ground forces.

This arrangement should not be visualized as a one-way street, for there are many things R.O.K. forces might do to help Japan, directly or indirectly. Such South Korean cooperation almost certainly would be limited to future air and naval cooperation with the U.S. as it defends Japan. Further in the future, it is conceivable that R.O.K. forces could cooperate with the U.S. in distant areas where South Korean interests were at stake. For example, had South Korea possessed the capabilities, it probably would have volunteered to help the U.S. in the Persian Gulf in 1987. If R.O.K. ground forces could be dispatched to Vietnam to help the U.S. aid a distant ally, in principle there should be no reason not to send some to neighboring Japan *if* they could be spared from South Korea's defense and were needed to defend against a Soviet threat? This prospect is almost certain to remain hypothetical because North Korea is unlikely to remain idle in those circumstances. If R.O.K. forces cannot be spared because of simultaneous dangers to South Korea, obviously their primary duty would remain national defense.

More likely, R.O.K. naval assistance in S.L.O.C. defenses should be contemplated for the future. This would benefit South Korea as much as the U.S. and Japan. The R.O.K.'s contemporary naval role is negligible. However, this can, and should, change. Because of the R.O.K.'s defacto insular location (i.e., water on three sides and no access on the fourth), South Korea functionally is an island in geopolitical and economic terms. It is highly dependent on the sea for its trade and strategic support. Consequently, South Korea has as much need to be involved in offshore air and S.L.O.C. defense in the region as the U.S. and Japan. Moreover, it increasingly possesses the financial and industrial means to become a viable partner in these missions. Still more likely, and central to the whole notion of regional security, is the prospect of both the R.O.K. and Japan helping the U.S. cope with the Soviet Union. Washington should more openly advocate discrete improvements in Japan-R.O.K.-U.S. security ties.

The U.S., without being crude, or undermining the confidence of either Tokyo or Seoul in the U.S. commitments to them, can nonetheless make clear to both that—while the United States' stake in Northeast Asia is a crucial one—it can never compare with their stakes in the security of their shared region. They *are* the region. It is no distant part of the world for them, as it is for Americans. Should U.S. interests in the region be disrupted, causing Americans to reduce their commitments, South Korea and Japan could not do the same. They must stand together in the face of an external threat or risk falling separately.

In this sense, Krauss' prescription cited earlier, for stimulating Japan's defense consciousness by allowing South Korean militarism to flourish, was misdirected. It might, of course, precipitate massive Japanese rearmament, but in a way that would leave our two allies as budding adversaries. That would do nothing to enhance regional stability or U.S. interests in that stability. Without the U.S., it also would be catastrophic for the R.O.K. and Japan, since each would still have to contend with the Soviet Union and North Korea. How much better if the U.S.—without diminishing its nuclear umbrella—could signal a desire to do slightly less for each ally in conventional terms, providing incentives for them to do slightly more for themselves and each other. As each ally assumed more self-defense burdens, the U.S. could turn its attention to defending security concerns that all three allies share to some extent but which only the U.S. as a superpower has the means to address. This includes nuclear strategy and far flung conventional defenses, such as in the Middle East.

The entire subject of U.S.-R.O.K.-Japan security trilateralism is considered so sensitive by many in all three countries that they consider it foolishly dangerous to even discuss it openly. Actually, the risks of leaving this hot issue unaddressed are far greater, making it more dangerous to avoid publicly addressing improved trilateral security cooperation. Instead of permitting frictions with the U.S., or with each other, to becloud their future, it is more prudent for Tokyo and Seoul to preempt such possibilities by cooperating with each other militarily under United States auspices on an incremental basis. For such measures to make a meaningful contribution to lasting security they should be based on a popularly accepted consensus in all three countries. Popular support for any trilateral cooperation presently is weak, at best. It needs to be strengthened in an open manner.

Instead of aggravating tensions, and threatening to undermine U.S. support for its Northeast Asian commitments, Tokyo and Seoul must view such cooperation as an insurance policy to assure regional peace and stability. Furthermore, it may open the way to a significantly larger Japanese and South Korean role in support of the United States' overall commitments. That would serve Japanese and South Korean strategic interests and ingratiate each of them in Washington's eyes, thereby helping to mellow the United States' trade frictions with each ally.

With a cautious but more purposeful policy and an appreciation of common threat perceptions, a willingness to cooperate with each other in trilateral fashion, and enhanced mutual respect for the others' interests and desires to participate in decisionmaking, the U.S. might create an atmosphere conducive to regional security consciousness. Though South Korea and Japan, in conjunction with the U.S., can cooperate more in military-related security matters, we must also note the great potential of these two allies to work harmoniously in tension-reduction initiatives.

South Koreans and Japanese are capable of great contributions to economic and political measures that could reduce tensions versus the Soviet Union, North Korea, Vietnam, and other—non-Asian— security concerns. Both can also make major contributions to enhanced stability in the region, and elsewhere, through economic development assistance. Japan's potential for economic contributions to peacemaking is, for obvious reasons, far larger than South Korea's. However, Seoul also has growing potential to help economically. While these capabilities should be welcomed by Americans, perhaps as part of trilateral comprehensive security, they should not become a substitute for what both allies can contribute militarily. This is especially true of Japan, most likely to try such a substitution. It is not fair for the Japanese to arrogate to themselves the easiest, least dangerous, and most profitable economic roles in regional security while the U.S. and R.O.K. undertake the more arduous tasks. The U.S., R.O.K., and Japan face shared dangers and should more fairly share the responsibility for them.

Restructuring the Combined Forces Command

If the U.S. pursues this strategy, in conjunction with a restructuring of its deployments in Korea, another facet of the U.S.-R.O.K. security relationship should be adjusted. As a starter the U.S.-R.O.K. Combined Forces Command should be restructured to enable the U.S. to achieve a lower political profile. Restructuring it is even more important for security purposes. The U.S., in cooperation with the R.O.K., should create a divided joint command structure. Though that might seem like a contradiction in terms, it is not. The C.F.C. should be divided in two, along functional strategic lines. One (C.F.C.-I) should be tasked with the local defense of South Korea, and the other (C.F.C.-II) should be tasked with providing for the regional defense of South Korea as part of a larger strategic network.

Those forces in South Korea responsible for ground defense, air support, and coastal naval defense against North Korean aggression should properly be under Korean command. This version of the C.F.C. would include the great majority of South Korean forces and a small contingent of U.S. forces which would cooperate with an R.O.K.-led C.F.C.-I. As the U.S. ground forces are restructured and replaced by R.O.K. forces, C.F.C.-I would become almost entirely South Korean, in terms of combat forces. As the R.O.K. meets its goals and becomes more self-reliant, the entire U.S. contingent could be phased out, except for intelligence, logistic, and liaison personnel. Those forces in the other C.F.C., oriented toward Korea's regional defenses, would include dual purpose ground and air elements, forces which provide for the U.S. nuclear umbrella

78

in Northeast Asia, and bluewater naval components. Today most of these forces are American, but in time South Korea can contribute more to such security in terms of conventional defenses, logistics, and repair facilities.

Some prominent South Korean defense intellectuals already contemplate these roles. With proper encouragement from the U.S., there are real prospects that South Korea can assume them. On balance, however, because of the need for complementarity with other U.S. regional forces, and because the U.S. presumably would provide the largest components of regional forces, C.F.C.-II should remain under U.S. command and operational control. Because C.F.C.-II would orchestrate U.S. regional assets in Korea, and provide liaison with other U.S. forces in the Western Pacific, with allied forces, and with the U.S.-affiliated global strategic network, it would greatly enhance South Korea's military contribution toward coping with the major threat behind its North Korean threat: namely, the Soviet Union.

The advantages of such a system would be great. The peninsular focus of C.F.C.-I would allow that organization to do nearly everything the current C.F.C. does but without its liabilities. Militarily, C.F.C.-I would take advantage of R.O.K. assets and allow R.O.K. forces to do what they do best. However, it would no longer affront Korean nationalistic sensitivities as the current C.F.C. frequently does. The appearance of political impropriety would be eliminated by not placing a U.S. officer in a command or control position, where he might be charged with sanctioning the R.O.K. military's suppression of domestic unrest and its intervention in politics, the civilian bureaucracy, and private sector business enterprises. Many Korean and American officials presently bemoan such appearances and seek ways to rectify them. The C.F.C.-II organizational structure would neither assault R.O.K. nationalism nor drag the U.S. into South Korean domestic politics. Instead, it would become part of a stronger tripwire for South Korea, enhancing Washington's guarantee to retain its commitment to the R.O.K. It also would open new strategic vistas for South Korean contributions to regional defenses (including cooperative actions against North Korea), enlarge South Korean prospects of interaction with other U.S. allies in the region, and demonstrate R.O.K. willingness to do what it can—primarily at sea and in the air—with the U.S. to deter the Soviet Union.

Further, C.F.C.-II would enlarge U.S. freedom of action within the region, to coordinate better its actions with activities in other regions, and to retain a firm grip on the nuclear umbrella. U.S. regional forces in Korea would not duplicate comparable forces elsewhere in Asia. They would supplement those other forces by a more efficient use of existing force levels in Korea. In addition to their availability in Korean contingencies, they could serve as rapid deployment forces region-wide. Certain units in C.F.C.-II could assume low-intensity conflict missions in the region. Moreover, their location in southern South Korea would be at the center of any East Asian conflict, with R.O.K. production and repair facilities to support their activities. Just as important, U.S. control of C.F.C.-II could ensure this without any suggestion of political impropriety, since R.O.K. elements in it would be offshore-focused and, by definition, not troops capable of meddling in Seoul politics. Riots are not readily controlled or coups staged with ships, missiles, aircraft, or rear area logistics troops.

There is an inherent civil-military danger in the C.F.C.-I proposal. Though many critics of the U.S.-led command structure have lambasted Washington for sanctioning the R.O.K. military's intervention in Korean politics, the proposal for separating the command arrangements will only partially relieve the problem. It would essentially solve the problem for the U.S. military because they would no longer be atop the hierarchy, but it would not eliminate the problem for South Korean society. Potential coupmakers could still stage a coup. In a sense, they would be under even fewer constraints, making coupmaking easier. This is a real danger, one that U.S. political and diplomatic leaders would have to address. The U.S. military command hierarchy in Seoul has unfairly been on a hot seat, seemingly all powerful, but actually less able to affect political decisions by their R.O.K. military counterparts than most Korean and American critics believe. On balance, the proposed of the C.F.C. would be strategically and politically beneficial for U.S. interests. It ought to be an intrinsic part of security reforms.

Nuclear Issues

Finally, attention is invited to two broader issues that are not specific only to Korea, but have a major impact on future U.S.-R.O.K. security relations. These are regional nuclear issues, and the role of U.S. forces in the Western Pacific in global U.S. strategy. U.S. nuclear policy toward Korea is a most delicate aspect of our overall policy. Precisely how the U.S. maintains its so-called nuclear umbrella over an ally should never be a subject for public debate. The U.S. maintains silence, in the case of South Korea, as it does in all other alliances. Nevertheless, there are aspects of this policy area that should be openly discussed. Worth questioning is the wisdom of the U.S. and the R.O.K. exerting leverage over each other because one is a nuclear-armed superpower opposing nuclear proliferation and the other is a small potential nuclear power. It would improve bilateral defense and overall relations if that subtle source of tension could be eliminated by Seoul and Washington after reaching a mutual position on nuclear nonproliferation in exchange for U.S. assurances to the R.O.K. of a deep and lasting commitment. That would be facilitated by a U.S. shift toward assuming Korea-based regional roles. However, a more specific understanding, based on a popular consensus, would be worthwhile. The U.S. should pursue with South Korea a more explicit, and popularly accepted, solution on nuclear policy suitable to both that could strengthen popular support for the alliance in both countries. This issue is particularly important in Korea where the nuclear umbrella notion is often misperceived by critics of U.S. strategy as excessively one-sided and constraining to South Korea.

Equally important, the U.S. and R.O.K. should pay more attention to meshing their policies toward nuclear disarmament. The Soviet Union frequently presses for nuclear free zones, whose appeal is great. New Zealand's anti-nuclear stance, Japan's "Three Non-nuclear Principles," and Southeast Asian support for the Z.O.P.F.A.N. (Zone Of Peace, Freedom, And Neutrality) all represent corresponding ideas in the non-communist world. Asians must recognize, as must Europeans, what the denuclearization of their region might mean in terms of conventionally armed security issues. With less fear of nuclear holocaust by theater nuclear weapons, and their potential for lowering the global nuclear war threshold, it is easier to visualize regional conflict escalation and national risk-taking. A number of Asian states—the U.S.S.R., China, Japan, India, Vietnam, Indonesia, and both Koreas—are major conventionally armed powers. The two Korean adversaries might be severely affected by a denuclearized Asia.

Pyongyang probably would be less intimidated by R.O.K.-U.S. deterrence under circumstances in which U.S. nuclear retaliation for a conventional North Korean attack on South Korea no longer need be feared. The South Korean situation would echo N.A.T.O.'s concerns about the Warsaw Pact's conventional arms advantages. Asian denuclearization may never occur but, in preparation for it, the U.S. should consider consulting with South Korea (and Japan and China) to develop contingency plans. Such plans might entail a massive conventional buildup. It would be far wiser, however, to emphasize tension-reduction measures to preempt any new and costly conventional arms race. Foremost should be a Korean version of the "MBFR" (Mutual and Balanced Force Reduction) talks in Europe. If they occur, U.S. forces in Korea should become a bargaining chip in such negotiations. Neither Seoul nor Washington should shy away from that prospect if verifiable agreements seem feasible.

Korea's Place In Global Strategy

If considering conventional war in a denuclearized Asia raises troubling scenarios, considering a possible multi-theater conventional war is even more disturbing. The swing strategy was long ago shelved, officially and in theory. All the rhetoric espousing Asia's new importance to the U.S. presumably has reassured Asians about the end of the swing strategy. However, the swing strategy was not relegated to the junk heap primarily because it was seen as unwise in light of Asia's importance, but because there is little in the U.S. inventory in Asia to draw upon. U.S. forces are spread as thin in Asia as in some other areas outside Europe. This is the core reason for regional burdensharing.

Most American strategists remain preoccupied with the N.A.T.O. central front. Europe remains their primary concern because they perceive it as Moscow's primary focus. Hence U.S. concerns about the central front, the North and Barents Seas, the Mediterranean region, and the Middle East, loom much larger than most of Asia. Except for Japan, Asia seems to many U.S. strategists a theater in which to counterattack or to practice. Americans may not seriously contemplate drawing down U.S. forces in Asia to help out in Europe, but neither are we prepared to shift forces from Europe to Asia. Nor are forces dedicated to European contingencies likely to be shifted to Asia. In a major war, U.S. forces in Asia can be expected to act as a strategic complement to Europe—attacking to distract the Soviet Union from its western front. Does anyone think the reverse is true? Can one visualize the U.S. attacking in Europe to lure the Soviet Union away from a war that might start in Asia? Even in the case of a Japan- or China-focused war, this seems impossible given the strategic priorities commonly assigned by Americans to Europe.

Thus, two approaches should be taken in U.S.-R.O.K. security relations. One, for the short term, is to reemphasize the degree to which R.O.K. forces and U.S forces in Korea (and elsewhere in Asia) are self-reliant. Though there is no point in reviving the controversy generated by past remarks about U.S. troops in Korea learning to swim because they will not be reinforced, greater efforts are needed in planning for Northeast Asian contingencies in a multi-theater conventional war environment. If such planning for a multi-theater conflict is not done in a manner that would assure U.S. support for South Korea, the risks of being caught short-handed are increased. If the U.S. is unable to meet its commitments to South Korea using conventional forces, this would increase the terrible risks of inching towards a U.S. nuclear option.

The second approach should be a longer term effort to convince U.S. strategists that Asia—especially Northeast Asia—is every bit as important as Western Europe, and deserves comparable attention. The assumed differentials in quality and quantity between Western Europe and Northeast Asia are no longer so valid as reasons for putting Europe first. Northeast Asia should not be treated as a second-class strategic theater. Americans should—in principle—be as prepared to counterattack in Europe, or in the Middle East, to save Asia as we are to use Asia as strategic leverage to meet U.S. goals in Europe. Realistically, that principle is not credible. However, U.S. willingness to treat Asia as strategic leverage should not be considered credible either.

Neither group of allies should be considered pawns for the strategic benefit of the other. However, such a balanced view cannot be achieved if Americans continue to consider Asia an appropriate site for a strategic ploy. Our Northeast Asian allies do not want to be pawns on a NATO chess board any more than Western Europeans would be willing to be strategic pawns to distract from a hypothetical attack on U.S. allies in Northeast Asia. The feelings of many South Koreans and Japanese on this issue are strongly held. They want to be treated on a rough par with Europeans. Unfortunately, the U.S. is far from treating these two regions with even a semblance of parity. In time, if security burdens and decision-making authority are shared in each region, Northeast Asian views of their region should achieve parity with European views of their's in the calculations of U.S. policymakers.

Such a goal may seem illusive now, but it is not impossible. Neither are any of the other suggestions for improved bilateral or regional security relations raised here. They can be achieved if the U.S. presses firmly enough. South Korea has the potential for becoming a truly "vital" ally. It possesses skilled military manpower, a dynamic economy, and a geopolitically important location. In addition to coping with North Korea, U.S.-R.O.K. military cooperation could become regionally important. The South Korean economy has significant potential as an arms production partner for the U.S., including the next generation of high-tech smart weapons. As important, South Korea's leaders are ready, willing, and able to cooperate with the United States in many ways. Whether the specific security proposals made here are implemented or not, the message behind them remains important. Some change is inevitable, but it is better that the change meet global and regional U.S.

interests, be systematic rather than ad hoc, and be compatible with other changes occurring in Korea and its environs.

Political Recommendations

Before considering recommendations for U.S. policy toward Korean political issues, let us briefly examine three social factors that bear on U.S.-Korean relations.

The growth of the Korean-American ethnic community since the 1960s has been phenomenal. There are approximately one million Americans of Korean heritage. Washington should try to use more effectively the assets this American ethnic community can provide for U.S.-Korean relations. It should also be more sensitive to the Korean-American community's feelings for their ancestral homeland and interest in U.S. policy toward Korea.

Another ethnic group also deserves more attention than it now receives—Amerasians in Korea. Though support in the U.S. is virtually nil for emphasizing the cause of Amerasians in human rights policy, morally they deserve the highest priority. One can only hope that a future administration will assign these frequently forgotten half-Americans—left behind in several Asian countries—the humanitarian assistance which should be their birthright. Their neglect by the U.S. is a disgrace.

The third domestic societal issue is the role of the "Moonies." The Reverend Moon Sun-myung's organization has been extraordinarily controversial in the U.S. for years. Its religious, business, academic, and publishing activities in the U.S. draw unusually negative attention to South Korea's relations with the United States. Though the Moon organization—and its several offshoots—engage in legitimate endeavors, their reputation is mixed. Their image is redolent of the Koreagate era. When a more liberal U.S. administration takes office, it may be less tolerant of the Moon organizations' efforts on behalf of ultra-conservative causes in the U.S. that favor South Korea. This could cause additional problems for U.S.-R.O.K. relations, and Washington should be sensitive to that potential.

Korean Political Developments

Shifting from U.S. policy toward political events affecting the U.S., let us consider recommendations for U.S. policy toward South Korean political developments.

Washington has been congratulating itself since mid-1987, when Roh Tae-woo set in motion a new wave of high expectations for South Korean democratic pluralism. The events of late 1987, while rough in spots, tended to confirm this optimism. Despite the complaints of the losers, the election of Roh as president appears to have put South Korea on the first rung toward real democracy. The Roh government moved rapidly to reduce the repressive policies of its predecessors. Roh personally seems committed to making his government more accessible to the South Korean masses. He has made significant progress in bringing democracy to a nation which long sought it but still is uncertain how to make it work. However, South Korea's earlier track record is not good enough to warrant optimism that Seoul can readily turn over a new leaf. South Korea has a long way to go before it is politically stable. The period surrounding the 1988 Summer Olympics is likely to test that stability because of dangers of more internal unrest and North Korean disruptions. In addition, the legacy of Kwangju still lingers, making Roh's task doubly difficult. Kwangju also casts a dark shadow over U.S. policy toward South Korean political developments. Consequently, it is important to determine how the U.S. can help South Korean democratic pluralism flourish.

The most basic reform needed in U.S. policy toward South Korean politics is to change American attitudes, injecting a sorely needed dose of humility. The U.S. government (executive and legislative branches) and American critics of U.S. human rights policies toward Korea have displayed a certain intellectual arrogance toward each other and events in Korea. Both seem to "know what's best," one tending towards benign neglect, and the other towards vocal activism. Each approach has limited virtues, but a fundamentally different attitude would be more appropriate. Americans should drop their cocky confidence about knowing what is best for Koreans, and should stop explaining to each other what is good for Korea.

The U.S. has lost the limited ability it once enjoyed to control political developments in South Korea. Instead of mourning that loss, or trying to reestablish U.S. controls, Americans should be happy that South Korea has matured, and no longer needs an American mentor. The U.S. should welcome these changes as an opportunity to correct false South Korean perceptions that the U.S. props up and manipulates "puppets" in a "client state." Except for discretely business-oriented lobbying efforts, the U.S. should distance itself from the convoluted Confucian workings of South Korean politics, remaining a highly interested bystander. However, should Korean politics sour again, the U.S. ought not be, or even appear to be, so committed to South Korean political leaders that their success or failure could be laid at the feet of the U.S. Though it is South Korea's closest security and economic partner, the U.S. should do everything it can to turn the political spotlight away from itself. This is especially important because of the nationalistic pride that the Seoul Olympics is likely to reinforce and, to some extent, exacerbate. Adopting security and economic policies toward Korea which better serve U.S. interests will help that process, but Washington also must do more to distance itself from the Seoul leadership's narrow political ambitions.

While the U.S. benignly distances itself from the parochial interests of individual political leaders in Seoul (by avoiding effusive praise of South Korean political leaders or unduly enthusiastic welcomes for R.O.K. politicians who visit the U.S.), the U.S. could nonetheless be more active in public and private pressures for systematic reforms. This is not contradictory. The U.S. must seek the correct balance between supporting systemic reform and keeping its distance from Seoul's political infighting, without being so aloof from politicians who support reform that it could signal a lack of sympathy for their goals. Washington should remember its mistakes from the Chang Myun era, when it did not strike a proper balance between support for systemic reforms and advocates of reforms, and not repeat them.

The U.S. should be a *catalyst* for Korean democracy. In other words, like any catalyst, the U.S. should remain distinctly apart from the processes of change yet be a facilitating agent for change.

It should support the reformers' broad quest for reforms, but not their narrow quest for political office. Washington may have lost its ability to fashion Seoul politics, but it can still exert positive influence over the processes involved. Moreover, as in security and economic affairs, the U.S. ought to use its available leverage while it remains viable. Washington, politically and through its human rights policy, should use all its influence to nudge South Koreans toward expanding political dialogue and cooperation. Though factionalism is, and probably will remain, endemic in South Korean politics, it can be overcome in certain circumstances. Americans should remind contentious Koreans of their folk proverb, "Even a sheet of paper is lighter when two people lift it."

If the U.S. is to rely on the R.O.K. as a regionally important ally and globally important trade partner, it cannot tolerate political excesses in Seoul. Hence, Washington should make clear, in public and private, that its past tolerance of excesses for the sake of stability in a client state is wearing thin. If Seoul politicians are unwilling to compromise with each other, build a real consensus, and sustain popular support for the governments they form, they should have no illusions that Washington will implicitly sanction R.O.K. political excesses as it has in the past. If South Korea wants to be a mature partner of the U.S., it must behave like one or risk weakening the U.S. support it expects. South Korea is potentially part of a U.S.-led global strategic and economic network of states that reinforce and sustain each other. However, Washington should make it abundantly clear to Seoul that it will never become a truly vital part of that system should it be a politically weak link in the chain. The U.S. cannot coerce South Korea to aspire to such a role, or to behave like a strong link. South Koreans will make their own decisions as a sovereign people. However, Seoul must be prepared to live with the consequences of its decisions in terms of American reactions to them.

U.S. Leverage For Political Reform

In this broader context, not solely in terms of bilateral U.S. interests in South Korea, Washington should use its leverage over the R.O.K. as a catalyst for systematic political reforms chosen by the South Korean people. "Leverage" does not mean that the U.S. should use American security and economic relations to twist Seoul's arm politically. Washington could do that, and some Americans, notably in the Congress, advocate such leverage. This is a profligate approach, because U.S. interests in Korea, on the economic and security fronts, are too important to jeopardize for short-term, narrow political gains. Moreover, Seoul's reactions to heavy-handed U.S. pressures have been negative. It would only exacerbate anti-Americanism. More sophisticated forms of influence need to be used here, too.

Instead of threats to cut U.S. troops, or reduce R.O.K. access to the U.S. economy, the U.S. might well adopt a carrot-and-stick approach. If domestic political progress is made, Seoul's behavior should be rewarded with improved bilateral security and economic arrangements in the form of opportunities to share decisionmaking power more extensively. In exchange for demonstrable progress toward genuine political pluralism, the U.S. should offer South Korea equally genuine chances to increase its voice in joint decision-making councils. Similarly, to the extent South Korean political pluralism becomes well established, and stable, Seoul's arguments that it is dependent on popular support for its negotiating positions regarding economic and security issues will become more credible to American negotiators. In short, Washington should be more attentive to the views of Seoul when its officials can more accurately claim to represent the South Korean people.

If Seoul wants to take advantage of such opportunities, it should liberalize its political system, making it more pluralistic and open to competing forces as it has promised for years. The Roh government seems firmly on that track. However, if Seoul is unwilling to pursue that course, it should be denied U.S. help in strengthening R.O.K. security self-reliance, cooperation in meeting R.O.K. economic goals, and sympathy in its foreign relations. Should Seoul's authoritarianism persist in the face of domestic demands for pluralistic freedoms and U.S. pressures for systematic reforms, it must realize that it will pay a stiff price in lost opportunities to obtain American compassion for South Korean positions. Over time, such South Korean policies can be expected to leave a bitter taste among the American public. American activists then might legitimately ask whether harsher forms of U.S. leverage ought to be reconsidered.

Near-Term Measures

Against the overall background of these longer range recommendations, three more immediate issues should be addressed: what to do about the former government's leader, what to do if further military intervention in politics is incipient or actually occurs, and how to encourage the new government.

Chun Doo-hwan undoubtedly expects to remain a powerful behind-the-scenes figure, an elder statesman of some sort. Whether or not Chun personally manages to retain that degree of influence, the U.S. should do all it can to encourage the Roh government—as it pursues pluralistic political reforms—to keep its distance from the systemic excesses that Chun, and Park before him, represented. Seoul's new leaders need encouragement to identify strongly with the civilian traditions of Korea's political culture that have been usurped and trampled since 1961.

There are many actions the U.S. can, and should, take to deter or preempt military intervention in politics if serious instability reemerges under the Roh administration as outlined in the key issues section. Basic would be a campaign to stress to the R.O.K. military U.S. aversion to another coup or martial law. It is true that U.S. interests in Korea do not fluctuate with the character of the regime in power in Seoul, making acceptance of another military-backed clique theoretically acceptable. However, the prospect of increased anti-Americanism, stimulated by U.S. de facto sanctioning of another coup, could be highly damaging to U.S. ability to pursue its interests in Korea.

There must be a coordinated, broad U.S. effort—by politicians, diplomats, the military, scholars, and the business community—to exchange ideas with their Korean counterparts about the effects of another coup on U.S. confidence in the R.O.K. and its long range influence on future U.S.-R.O.K. relations. Americans should be emphatic about the dangers of a Korean version of a "banana republic." Beyond broad persuasive efforts, the R.O.K. military should be encouraged to expand its strategic horizons into regional security in cooperation with the U.S. As well as being intrinsically valid, that shift could also provide a major incentive for the R.O.K. military to seek larger roles for itself than would be possible if it reverted to coupmaking. Furthermore, by expanding into larger roles, the R.O.K. military would have to do two things that—as a fringe benefit—reduce the prospect of another coup. South Korean assumption of a larger regional security role would require the diversion of greater domestic resources to the R.O.K. Air Force and Navy, not normally the branches prone to devising coups. If strengthened, those far less politicized service branches may be able to influence their Army colleagues not to stage a coup. Concommitantly, the R.O.K. Army would become more dependent for its strategic backstop upon an interdependent U.S.-R.O.K. force structure which would not be as locked into automatic support for South Korea. This would tend to make it more difficult for the R.O.K. Army to lead a coup and thereby risk the American commitment to South Korea's security.

If military intervention occurs in spite of U.S. efforts, the United States must be prepared. The U.S. should send unmistakable signals to potential coupmakers that they cannot expect the degree of U.S. tolerance received by their predecessors. To underline U.S. seriousness about its unwillingness to accede once more, the U.S. should distance itself in advance from any system that might connote U.S. approval of another coup or martial law crackdown.

The U.S. should also signal what it would do if faced by another coup in Seoul. At that point, all the economic and strategic leverage available to the U.S. in South Korea ought to be employed for their deterrence value. Potential coupmakers in the R.O.K. army might be told that any move on their part to reverse the progress made toward stable democratic pluralism would bring about an automatic set of adverse U.S. responses including cuts in U.S. strategic support to South Korea and sharp restrictions on South Korean access to the U.S. economy. That message must come through loud and clear to latent coupmakers. If it does not, and a coup occurs,

Washington must keep its word and incrementally cut selected ties to Seoul until the situation is reversed. If coupmakers were to persist, they would have to face indefinite U.S. reluctance to return to "business as usual."

Assuming that the R.O.K. maintains some viable form of pluralistic politics, as now seems likely, Washington must be prepared to support that system. The Seoul leaderhip may not always be as cooperative with Americans as we have been accustomed to, may not be as disciplined as past regimes, and may not be as skilled at running the R.O.K. Americans must expect occasional rough times in U.S.-R.O.K. relations, when both Washington and Seoul have to answer to public pressures from their respective constituencies whose interests do not coincide. Without sacrificing important U.S. interests, Americans ought to be willing to pay some strategic and economic prices if necessary to help R.O.K. democratic leaders reinforce stability. If they need some symbolic concessions from the U.S. in order to sustain democracy in South Korea, the price should be considered by Washington. If we were willing to absorb some costs for the sake of building up an authoritarian R.O.K. militarily and economically, there is no reason not to pay comparable costs to encourage popularly supported democratic pluralism which promises to make the contemporary R.O.K. an even more important ally and trade partner. Consequently, the U.S. should recognize that some security and economic costs, in the form of American negotiating concessions, may be inescapable for the sake of U.S. support for continued political reforms.

The U.S. cannot control South Korea's political evolution, nor can it produce a mini-U.S. clone in South Korea. Even under a pluralistic system, there is a strong likelihood that South Koreans will not devise political standards which would pass muster under existing worldwide U.S. human rights criteria. That may *never* occur in Korea, and Americans must be prepared for that eventuality. We must not harbor unrealistic expectations that are certain to be dashed and cause new frustrations. Korean answers to the quest for freedom and pluralism can be as valid for Korean society as American answers are for U.S. society. We must shed our chauvinism in such matters. There is no "Made In U.S.A." model political culture that Americans should expect to see replicated in South Korea.

U.S. Policy Toward North Korea

The final set of policy recommendations deals with U.S. policy toward North Korea which is worthy of more attention. The substantial progress toward an innovative diplomatic and trade policy toward North Korea, made under the Reagan-Shultz-Sigur-Walker/ Lilley team, deserves a great deal of credit. However, their moves were only cautious first steps, and should be followed by greater innovation.

In an upbeat July 1987 speech before the Foreign Policy Association, Assistant Secretary Sigur, quoting the American equivalent of a Korean saying, "Well begun is half done," spoke positively of the prospects for R.O.K.-D.P.R.K. reconciliation. North-South tension-reduction should continue to be a significant portion of U.S. policy toward Korea. However, that saying—*shijag i ban ida*—is more appropriate in a realm where the U.S. has real control: its own policy toward North Korea. Washington's move off dead center in its contacts with Pyongyang was, indeed, a matter of "well begun" being major progress. "Smile diplomacy" was again in full grimace, with clenched teeth. U.S. diplomats reportedly met informally with their North Korean counterparts in Europe and Africa, though with few evident results. The U.S. also displayed new flexibility toward North Korean travel in the United States.

North Korea's responses to revived U.S. attention were more positive than in the first iteration. Pyongyang formally "welcomed" the U.S. moves, though it insisted Washington's actions did not really toss the ball into North Korea's court. The Kim regime pressed for more concrete action. It wants what the U.S. and R.O.K. will not, and should not, give: namely, the withdrawal of U.S. forces from Korea or—in the interim—cessation of joint military exercises such "Team Spirit." It also wants the U.S. to agree to tripartite talks between the D.P.R.K. and U.S./R.O.K. This, too, is a poor idea because it places South Korea in an unequal position.

93

In such talks only Pyongyang could claim to be representing Korea independently. Unfortunately, the tripartite notion was first raised by Americans which makes it awkward to reject now that North Korea wants it. Nevertheless, it remains a poor idea which should be avoided.

It is no surprise that U.S./D.P.R.K. feelers produced little movement. Neither were strongly motivated. Washington's denunciation of North Korea as a terrorist state in January 1988 halted those tenuous moves. The second wave of "smile diplomacy" was aborted. Once again, U.S.-North Korean relations were chilled. Frown diplomacy was back in style. North Korea's hatred of the U.S., and Pyongyang's paranoia, run deep. It has raised these sentiments to something approaching an art form.

The D.P.R.K. projects an abominable image for Americans because of its involvement in the D.M.Z. axe murders, the Pueblo incident, and other notorious events. Furthermore, North Korea is widely considered an international renegade because of its support for terrorists and radical revolutionaries. Pyongyang's vituperous attacks on the U.S. are onerous for Americans, partly because they are incredibly obtuse, but mainly because they do not reflect any realistic understanding of American motives. All sorts of heinous purposes are ascribed to the U.S., making it extraordinarily difficult for Americans to be either civil toward, or objective about, North Koreans. Accordingly, Americans often assume substantial irrationality prevails in Pyongyang, and act on that assumption.

While Washington had to display diplomatic solidarity with Seoul, by signaling its anger at Pyongyang's renewed support for terrorism in 1987, U.S. policy has reverted to futile gestures. Something needs to be done to break this pattern of distrust and tension. The U.S., after a suitable—but short—interval, should take the initiative again. An appropriate time might be in 1989 after a new U.S. administration is in office and the impact of the Olympics can be assessed. South Korea long has advocated proposals for concurrent and simultaneous cross recognition. These have miscarried. Despite periodic North-South talks, and some progress, the two Koreas remain bitter adversaries. South Korea fears deeply that the U.S., or Japan might break ranks and deal directly with North Korea. U.S. "smile diplomacy" led Seoul to exert pressures on the U.S. not to progress too far too fast. Seoul is pleased that the effort to thaw relations has been derailed again. While South Korean concerns are understandable, it is in the United States' interests to be more innovative. The U.S. should prudently proceed much further and faster than Seoul wants. "Smile diploacy" should be reactivated and expanded in a prudent manner.

South Korea's attitude amounts to a demand for a unit veto over U.S. policy options. While Seoul says it has no control over U.S. policy, in practice, it assumes the right indirectly to approve or disapprove any policy the U.S. might consider toward North Korea. While being careful not to be too blunt, or to offend Americans, Seoul presumes Washington usually will rubber stamp South Korean policies toward North Korea. This frequently has been the case; thus U.S. options toward North Korea have been minimal. At the same time South Korea feels totally free to experiment diplomatically and economically with the P.R.C., U.S.S.R., North Korea and other communist states. This is part of Seoul's adaptation of Tokyo's omnidirectional foreign policy and is a wise posture for South Korea. Seoul expects its ties with the P.R.C. and U.S.S.R. to take off after the 1988 Olympics. In that context, Roh Tae-woo felt no inhibitions about promising, during the 1987 campaign, to pursue greatly expanded R.O.K.-P.R.C. relations.

Were an American presidential candidate to make a similar pledge about U.S.-D.P.R.K. relations, most South Koreans would be aghast. Seoul disapproves of any serious U.S. approaches to North Korea that are not conditioned by South Korean restrictions. In effect, Seoul maintains a diplomatic double standard: what exalts the South Korean goose is not good for the U.S. gander. The U.S. should reject this South Korean assumption strongly and openly. This does not, of course, mean that the U.S. should oppose R.O.K. overtures to China and the Soviet Union. Far from it: they suit U.S. interests in tension-reduction almost as well as South Korean interests. However, the U.S. should retain the same latitude in its relations with North Korea.

The U.S. can deal with North Korea without having to get Seoul's approval in advance. To accept Seoul's implicit "veto" yields a sovereign right. Taking this position does not mean that the U.S. should treat with North Korea behind South Korea's back, merely to make its point. That would be shortsighted and inane. Neither does it mean that the U.S. should rush formally to recognize North Korea, which would signal to Pyongyang a serious weakening of U.S.-R.O.K. relations. As this study makes clear, there are major reasons for the U.S. to maintain and strengthen the bonds between the U.S. and South Korea. However, none of these reasons should exlude or prevent the U.S. from seriously considering some forms of improved U.S.-D.P.R.K. relations.

The United States should take advantage of its diplomatic assets in dealing with North Korea. The P.R.C. may want greatly to improve its ties with the R.O.K., but it cannot easily do so because of the D.P.R.K.'s ability to cast its lot with the U.S.S.R. The Soviet Union is less interested in improving U.S.S.R.-R.O.K. ties, but— should it contemplate doing so—Pyongyang's China card remains an obstacle. Of course, both the P.R.C. and U.S.S.R. could improve relations with the R.O.K. in tandem, without allowing North Korea a veto, but that is an improbable scenario. Japan might initiate a rapid improvement in its relations with the D.P.R.K., but only at the cost of seriously damaging its ties with South Korea and provoking the pro-R.O.K. Korean minority in Japan. Only the U.S.—if it explains its moves properly—has the latitude to improve its ties with its Korean adversary without losing the allegiance of its Korean ally.

While the U.S. should not foreclose the possibility of multilateral talks on Korean tension-reduction and unification, they do not hold much promise of success. Washington should consult with Seoul about the potentials for such talks, but it also must consider separate U.S. options. The U.S. should prepare itself substantively for the day that formal relations with North Korea become feasible. The U.S. does not now expect, or openly plan for, such relations. This is a mistake. Without doing an end-run around South Korea, or reneging on numerous promises to Seoul, the U.S. should make contingency plans for improved U.S.-D.P.R.K. relations and acknowledge their existence openly.

The U.S. needs to be more sensitive to North Korea's security concerns, learn more about its economic motivation, and be more objective about North Korea's position in the international system. We should try to understand North Korea's hatred of the U.S. for its support of South Korea, why it despises the United States' role in the world, and the depth of its paranoia about the United States' ability to attack North Korea. This can be facilitated by expanding American knowledge of North Korea and understanding of Pyongyang's point of view. An increased effort by Americans to understand North Korea's actions would help the U.S. to craft policies that may be able to reduce tensions in Korea. North Korea has made several significant proposals on arms control which the U.S. writes off as propaganda. Much of it *is* propaganda, but the U.S. should be prepared to call North Korea's bluff and—in cooperation with South Korea—test Pyongyang's willingness to follow up its words with action.

North Korea is a complex society. Though run by a dictator, there are other centers of power. The U.S. should try harder to influence these other centers of power, directly and indirectly. Those centers are being affected by generational changes as better educated, more sophisticated, and more technocratic individuals assume positions of authority. The imminent succession of Kim Jong-il may mean a more approachable regime will run North Korea. Chinese, Soviet, and some American specialists on North Korea suggest this possibility. A second Kim regime may, of course, also mean a continuation of recycled Kim-ism with its inherent dangers. No responsible U.S. official can rely on the optimistic forecasts.

The U.S. should prepare itself for either possibility. It should stand by South Korea, ready to help if the worst case strategic scenarios are realized. Kim Jong-il may feel pressured to prove himself tough when he succeeds his father, leading to heightened danger of war on the peninsula. On the other hand, if the next North Korean regime proves to be more approachable, the U.S. must be prepared for that, too. The U.S. should be ready to adapt diplomatically, economically, and militarily to positive changes in North Korea if they materialize. The United States' contemporary position vis-a-vis North Korea is too rigid. It should be altered to allow whatever flexibility is needed to respond to positive—as well as negative—changes in North Korea.

South Korea already has incorporated such flexibility into its foreign policy regarding the Soviet Union and China. The U.S. should openly emulate South Korea's example. President Roh has gone so far as to say, in the Fall of 1987, that the R.O.K. would not object to the U.S. or Japan moving first on diplomatic cross recognition, if reciprocity from the U.S.S.R. or P.R.C. were guaranteed in advance. The U.S. should pursue that idea with the Roh government, aiming perhaps at a joint U.S.-R.O.K. initiative. Similarly, the U.S. should keep a very close eye on Roh's efforts to improve Seoul's relations with Beijing and Moscow. Washington does, and should, encourage such steps enthusiastically. Further, it should use improved U.S.-P.R.C. and U.S.-U.S.S.R. relations as a background against which American "good offices" on South Korea's behalf may be more effective. Perhaps most important, the U.S. should not be caught napping if South Korea succeeds diplomatically with China and/or the Soviet Union. The U.S. should maintain diplomatic contingency plans, ready to respond quickly in the U.S.-D.P.R.K. context.

In a sense the U.S. is trapped by its own past and present commitments to South Korea. In principle, the U.S. should proclaim its right to pursue whatever policy it chooses regarding North Korea. However, it has forfeited that prerogative to Seoul's implicit "veto." Continued U.S. support for Seoul's diplomatic position versus North Korea is sound, but the way in which the U.S. is providing that support is troubling.

The U.S. strongly supports South Korea's unification stance, but there are valid reasons for Americans to be skeptical about those positions. U.S. and R.O.K. interests in security, politics, and economics are not identical. Hence, it should surprise no one that we do not share identical interests on North-South Korean issues either. Moreover, Americans do not necessarily share with South Koreans a vision of what a unified Korea would mean for the region and the world beyond. Despite such differences, the U.S. permits the R.O.K. to circumscribe the parameters of U.S. options regarding North Korea.

Notwithstanding the ambiguity of current U.S. support for South Korea's unification agenda, the U.S. emphatically should not give up on prospects for unification. It may happen someday. In any event, it will only occur if the two Koreas want it badly enough to overcome their obstinacy. However, the United States should not expect unification any time soon. The most that is likely to emerge from North-South reunification talks is reduced tensions. This may be peripheral for unification-obsessed Koreans, but it could be a major advance for U.S. interests in Korea. The U.S. should expand its support for South Korean tension-reduction efforts.

Equally important, working closely with South Korea, the United States should pursue its own tension-reduction efforts regarding the Soviet Union and North Korea. This is the best way to minimize the need for the U.S. and its regional allies to confront the Soviet Union militarily. The U.S. can pursue reduced tensions by several means. One should be an expansion of non-strategic trade. South Korea is setting a precedent in its rapidly expanding trade with the P.R.C. which the U.S. should emulate with North Korea. There are some signs that North Korea is ready to open its economy more fully to the West. Our response is a test of our confidence in the virtues of capitalism. Perhaps we should offer North Korea a real opportunity to participate in the Pacific Basin economic network. If Pyongyang is at all interested in following the reformist examples of Deng's China or Gorbachev's Soviet Union, it should be given a chance.

Offering this opportunity should not be construed as a reward for past North Korean behavior, though Pyongyang's attitudes and policies during the 1988 Summer Olympics could be considered. More likely, however, such an overture should be considered an incentive for improved future behavior. It would also be worthwhile to pursue large scale cultural, scholarly, and scientific exchanges with North Korea. This would expose both societies to each other more thoroughly and enhance mutual understanding. Lastly, if the U.S. does restructure its security relationship with South Korea as suggested here, the U.S. should stress to Pyongyang that the primary focus of American security interests is the Soviet Union, not North Korea. Simultaneously, it should emphasize the potentials for U.S.-U.S.S.R. tension-reduction which would indirectly reduce North Korea's reasons to be concerned about its security.

Despite common misperceptions, North Korea is not a full-fledged Soviet surrogate. Nor do North Korea's close relations with China place it irrevocably in Beijing's orbit. North Korea is an independent actor—often too independent for the tastes of its allies and adversaries. Importantly, North Korea has shown it can be influenced by China and the Soviet Union. In recent years those influences have helped moderate North Korea's actions and should be encouraged. However, it may also be possible for the U.S., South Korea, and Japan to exert some positive influence over Pyongyang. There is no need for the U.S. to forfeit the game before Americans enter it. Washington should not allow North Korea's support for terrorism to become yet another reason for hardening U.S. policy. Such actions by Pyongyang should be considered reason for skillful innovation in U.S. policy, not an excuse for reversals. The U.S. objective should be to change North Korea's policies, not reinforce them. The U.S. should not write off North Korea as a lost cause, but should work diligently at eliminating barriers, reducing tensions, and building mutual confidence between the U.S. and the D.P.R.K.

4 Conclusion

Woven throughout this study is a consistent theme: the maturation of U.S.-R.O.K. relations. This process is accelerating rapidly. As Americans enter their fifth decade of relations with the Republic of Korea, the U.S. must cope with a markedly different country than the one born in the 1940s, ravaged by war and poverty. The revised priorities this study recommends accord well with dramatic changes in Korea and the U.S. South Korea has become a much more important country than it was when the U.S. extended commitments to the fledgling R.O.K. Though the U.S. stake in South Korea may one day achieve a magnitude warranting the description "vital interest," U.S. interests in Korea remain primarily derivative, predicated on regional concerns. However, those regional interests also are rapidly evolving. The emergence of Asian economic opportunities and challenges are truly new factors reshaping the international context within which U.S. foreign policy is crafted. Those factors are integral to the U.S.-R.O.K. relationship, transforming it before our eyes.

One consequence of this development is the necessity of pursuing seemingly paradoxical policies. The U.S. must work more closely with South Korea, and other Asian allies and trade partners, in pursuit of free market economic interdependence and strategic integration. At the same time, the U.S.—throughout Asia—must seek free and fair trade, mutually beneficial defense relationships, and political stability. These goals are likely to remain intact regardless of who occupies the White House. American politicians may approach these goals differently, but their basic objectives are similar. The U.S. must deal with Asian states on an unprecedented level of equality, but also stand up more assertively for its national interests than it has since 1945. U.S. foreign policy requires an odd mixture of American nationalism operating within an internationalist context.

As a result, a certain degree of ambiguity probably is unavoidable. The U.S. now is in its third cycle of ambiguity regarding Korea. Americans were ambiguous about Korea in the 1940s and 1960s for different reasons, but the 1980s version is just as potent. Though this mixture of feelings will require careful explanations, Americans need not be apologetic about asserting U.S. national interests within mature relationships because our Asian partners are at least as ambiguous about their involvement with the U.S. This certainly is true of South Korea's ties with the U.S. which embody all sorts of love-hate and inferiority-superiority complexes. Clearly, each partner needs to encourage a better understanding of the other, but that understanding must be a two-way street, displaying mutual empathy. Furthermore, South Korean frustrations with an increased American emphasis on U.S. national interests in Korean affairs, especially in trade, should be seen in a new light by Koreans and Americans.

Though South Koreans may resent what they see as a selfish and cold attitude on the part of Americans, they should recognize that the R.O.K. is now being treated objectively as a more ordinary country. Instead of being accorded special handling as an American protege, a newly powerful R.O.K. is being accorded the sort of treatment the U.S. dispenses to most of its allies and trade partners. In a somewhat perverse sense, South Korea is receiving from the U.S. the attention and respect it has earned. Americans should stress to South Koreans that the assertion of U.S. interests—sometimes at South Korea's expense—is a natural result of the R.O.K. becoming so important to the U.S. that Americans can no longer be as tolerant of South Korea impinging on U.S. interests. In effect, the R.O.K. formerly did not matter enough for the U.S. to exert substantial pressures on it; now it does. These realities may be difficult to accept, but—in time—South Koreans will learn to cope with the U.S. as well as other strong allies and trade partners do. After all, the benefits of this more equal partnership probably will be ample reward for South Koreans and Americans. The potentials inherent in mature U.S.-R.O.K. cooperation in economics, security, and politics are great. They should be viewed with anticipation, not apprehension.

Toward that end, Americans must show respect for Korean values, mores, problems and aspirations. In return, Koreans must show comparable respect for American values, mores, problems, and aspirations. If South Korea wants Washington to be a consistent supporter of its strategic, regional, political, and economic interests, Seoul must reciprocate in regard to the equivalent array of U.S. interests. The U.S. now confronts economic and security problems that can be partially ameliorated by appropriate cooperation by South Korea. Such "you scratch my back, I'll scratch your's" cooperation has not been a hallmark of U.S.-R.O.K. relations because South Korea rarely has been able to offer anything truly required by the U.S. That has changed dramatically, especially on the economic front where the U.S. is deadly serious about the urgency of obtaining fairness and breaking down barriers to U.S. exports which are an obstacle to the U.S. regaining its economic health.

Growing out of this national economic priority for the U.S. are a range of security and political objectives. The U.S. is overburdened strategically. It must either strengthen its capabilities, shed burdens, share burdens, or reduce the source of the threat causing the burdens to be borne. In Korea, the U.S. cannot rid itself of its burdens safely. There is little prospect that the U.S. will enlarge its capacity to meet existing commitments. Consequently, it must—in concert with allies—share responsibilities and try to find ways to minimize the dangers posed by the Soviet Union and North Korea.

Implicit in the recommended new priorities and policy alternatives for the U.S. in Korea is the concept of linkage. All facets of U.S. policy toward the two Koreas are inextricably linked. It is inappropriate to keep them artificially discrete. Security and economic linkages are the most crucial relationships emphasized in this study, but each of them is also tied closely to U.S. policy toward Korean politics and inter-Korean relations. Tinkering with one sector has repercussions in all the others. Similarly, letting problems fester in one sector will eventually cause repercussions in the others.

Linkage relationships mandate that U.S. policy become more coordinated and comprehensive.

Improving U.S. policy toward the two Koreas will not be quick or easy. There is a warranted sense of urgency about the problems the U.S. faces in Korea caused by a domestic economic requirement that the U.S. get its house in order if it is to remain a viable superpower. There is a real sense of urgency, but this does not mean that Americans should expect instant gratification as we are prone to do. We must not be unrealistically impatient. However, the pressures for change should not be unduly delayed because of excessive concern about their impact on Korea. Neither should any American predisposition toward hypercautious gradualism be given free rein. Koreans will slow down the United States' processes of policy change by their actions, Americans need not help them by voluntarily going slowly.

South Korea likes the skewed arrangements with the U.S. it has worked so assiduously for years to cultivate. It will do its utmost to preserve these arrangements. If there is to be change, Seoul obviously prefers that such changes more closely serve narrow R.O.K. interests. Most of the suggestions in this study should help both the U.S. and R.O.K., but because they are explicit in terms of what is best for the United States, they may arouse some resistance in South Korea. This is not surprising because there is unease in the U.S., too, about the wisdom of evolving U.S. relations with Asian economic challengers.

A number of significant changes may alter the uneven tenor of U.S.-Korean relations in the 1990s. In both Washington and Seoul new leaders will be in office. The American leader may be part of a post-World War II generation that is reshaping U.S. societal attitudes. Even if he is not actually part of the postwar generation, the new age group's worldview will be reflected in U.S. policy more than ever. Moreover, many of the policymakers in Washington inevitably will be of that generation.

Seoul's leadership is not expected to undergo such dramatic changes, but in South Korea, too, there is a pronounced generational change. Many young and early middle-aged Koreans have no strong memories of the Korean War. They often do not share the intense gratitude of their elders for what the U.S. did to help South Korea survive and prosper.

North Korea, too, is experiencing a generational change. Pyongyang's heir-designate may recite anti-American rhetoric, but not because he shared the same personal experiences as his father. However, the North's generational shift perhaps enhances the significance of weakened North Korean memories of Chinese help versus more recent Soviet assistance. That should concern Americans, too, but our prime concern should focus on the changing memories and perceptions of South Koreans and Americans.

Koreans have many proverbs, some heuristically useful for the policy issues raised in these recommendations. One of them evokes much that is relevant to generational changes in the U.S. and South Korea—"the frog does not remember its days as a tadpole." Americans who designed and carried out U.S. policy toward Korea since the 1940s often are annoyed by the failure of their Korean counterparts to transmit the older generation's understanding of, and appreciation for, U.S. aid and support for the R.O.K. in the 1940s, '50s, and '60s. Those older Koreans are equally upset at their inability to convey to the younger generation the feelings that have reinforced U.S.-R.O.K. bonds through the years. Clearly, these young South Koreans scarcely recall being "tadpoles," much less feel gratitude for whoever protected them while they and their country matured. Scarcely recognized by either older or younger Koreans, or by the older generation of American Korea-policymakers, is the equally casual attitude of young Americans toward Korean successes. If young Koreans are not especially grateful for past American deeds that are "history," as far as they are concerned, their American counterparts do not feel they are owed gratitude for what their parents or grandparents did for South Korea. For them, too, the Korean War is history. There are forgetful former tadpoles in both countries, soon to be leading them.

In the largest sense, this parallel emergence of different attitudes is healthy because it denotes a sharp reduction in the clientitis that mars both sides of the relationship. As these dual positive/negative memories fade, they should produce more mutual respect and objectivity in the relationship. Unfortunately, until sufficient time does pass, the younger generation of Americans now assuming political and economic power in the United States is likely to be more influential in U.S. policymaking than their South Korean counterparts on Korean policymaking and little empathy is felt by the post-Korean War generation in the U.S. for the verities keeping the U.S. commitment to South Korea intact for years.

Just as younger Koreans express their frustration with U.S. economic pressures on the R.O.K., and its apparent support for Seoul regimes they criticized as repressive, in sentiments that often are anti-American, many younger Americans share views which can be regarded as "anti-Korean." Actually, these views are rarely directed at Korea itself but rather at the general phenomena into which South Korea fits. There is an old, recurrent strain of isolationist and America-first attitudes that seems to be reemerging in the United States.

The current roots of this phenomenon are diffuse. They include: frustration with the insanity of nuclear confrontation; annoyance with allies in Europe and Asia who do not fully pull their own weight (not the R.O.K., but this exception is often overlooked); and an identification with the Vietnam syndrome, the formative event of this generation (comparable to the influence of opposition to Munich-like appeasement and support for postwar collective security upon the previous generation). They also share an inward-focused preoccupation with self-satisfaction characterized by the "yuppies" sub-group, and—perversely—a deep-seated anxiety that the so-called "American Dream" for the new generation is undermined by a foreign economic challenge—especially from Asia. Collectively, these attitudes may impair U.S. relations with Korea.

In effect, the United States is being "Americanized" by its domestic problems and the challenge of sustaining its superpower status. This, in turn, is leading to the Europeanization of the United States' Western European allies and trade partners—by which they look more to their own interests and capabilities. The "Asianization" of Asia has not yet happened in similar terms but it may. Ironically, a cause of Europeanization vs. Americanization—that is straining, and threatening to "decouple," the N.A.T.O. alliance and

Atlanticism—is the rise of the Pacific region as an economic center of global activities. The shift in focus of U.S. trade from the Atlantic to the Pacific was a benchmark in this transformation, causing anxiety among the United States' European allies. What remains uncertain is whether the reduction of Atlantic influence will be compensated by an accent on the Pacific. Despite much discussion of a Pacific community, Pacific basin, or Pacific rim network of shared interests—nothing in the Pacific approaches the cohesive qualities of the North Atlantic.

Currently, the U.S. is undergoing a transition which is unlikely to go full cycle. It is experiencing second thoughts about the degree of U.S.-led collective security in Europe, more than forty years after that system took shape. However, those reservations lack the strength seriously to jeopardize those arrangements. Americans have experienced such doubts before, but never have they been so openly expressed, or echoed in Europe with such resonance. Also making this iteration different is the partial economic shift toward the Pacific, causing Americans to reconsider some longstanding assumptions about the United States' fundamental orientation toward the East Coast and its ties to Europe. Because of growing Asia-Pacific economic ties, the West Coast's emergence as a viable and—in some areas—most advanced portion of the U.S. economy, and significant increases in the number and roles of Asian-Americans, the United States now looks across the Pacific as often as it does the Atlantic to determine its national interests.

The United States is in flux, somewhat uncertain where its main external affinities really lie. Because most Americans are of European extraction, and U.S. society is solidly rooted in Judeo-Christian values, the ties across the Atlantic are not based merely on objective criteria but on blood and heritage. Those ties will endure. However, Americans also have major ethnic ties to Africa, Asia, and Latin America. Though foreign officials often stereotype "Americans" as those of European background because of U.S. racial history, such views are obviously wrong in the 1980s. People of many backgrounds are being Americanized as never before, but without having to jettison their diverse heritage. As the U.S. progresses, it will incorporate the diversity of its peoples into bridges to other

parts of the world as Euroamericans have long done to Europe.
What does this mean for U.S. policy toward Korea? All the problem areas in U.S.-Korean relations, mentioned earlier, need
attention—some urgently. However, with the U.S. experiencing a
major societal, political, and economic transformation, it may be
more difficult than usual for it to create a consistent policy. The
changed perspectives of Americans of different generations also
will make U.S. policymaking more confusing to Koreans (and other
foreigners) than it is. They must try to understand what the U.S.
is undergoing. To ease ourselves through this trying change, and
help foreigners comprehend us, Americans should redouble their
efforts at enunciating clear and consistent policies. This is crucial
for a successful Korea policy.

As the U.S. confronts Korea in the future, one factor seems certain. It will be dealing with a nation whose importance for Americans can no longer be relegated to the fringe of U.S. concerns. Korea
may never become a central focus of U.S. policy. However, because
of Asia's increasing economic prominence—and Korea's role as a
geopolitical nexus—the peninsula promises to occupy a much larger
niche in Americans' consciousness. Consequently, all aspects of
U.S. policy toward Korea are likely to become more important in
the 1990s, and beyond, than is readily visualized by Americans
in 1988.

The new importance of Korea is symbolized by the 1988 Summer Olympics, coming only forty years after the Republic of Korea's
founding. Many South Koreans see these games as their equivalent of the 1964 Olympics in Japan. They expect the Olympics to
give South Korea a new and improved identity. Some of the political, economic, and security hopes and potential problems visualized for the Seoul Olympics have been addressed in this study. The
Olympics have the potential for elevating South Korea's stature if
they go well. National pride and hubris will be a major factor in
dealing with South Korea in the post-Olympics era. South Koreans
will be less tolerant of those Americans who still try to treat the
R.O.K. as a client state. While the post-Olympic attitudes of South
Koreans could become the basis for greater R.O.K. self-confidence
and improved cooperation with the U.S., Americans must expect

some prideful "arrogance" from their Korean counterparts. The Olympics also could damage South Korea's image should they not fare so well because of internal or external disruptions. In either event, the aura surrounding the Olympics will likely influence the near future of U.S.-Korea relations. For better or worse, the Korean Olympics—and issues associated with Korea—will cause many Americans to focus on Korea in unprecedented ways. U.S. policy toward Korea will, in turn, likely receive new attention by many Americans.

That policy, and its interaction with the responses and initiatives of the two Koreas, will shape future U.S.-Korea relations. One can only hope that Americans and Koreans will face the future with mutual respect and empathy so that our ties may achieve the real harmony eluding us in the 1980s.

RECOMMENDED READINGS

Barnds, William K., Ed. *The Two Koreas in East Asian Affairs.* New York: New York University Press, 1976.

Bandow, Doug, "Korea: The Case for Disengagement," *Policy Analysis*, No. 96, Washington, D.C., The CATO Institute, December 8, 1987.

Baldwin, Frank P. Jr., Ed., *Without Parallel: The American-Korean Relationship Since 1945.* New York: Pantheon Books, 1974.

Boettcher, Robert. *Gifts of Deceit: Sun Myung Moon, Tongsun Park and the Korean Scandal.* New York: Holt, Rinehart, and Winston, 1980.

Buss, Claude A. *The United States and The Republic of Korea; Background for Policy.* Stanford: Hoover Institution Press, 1982.

Central Intelligence Agency. *Korea: The Economic Race Between the North and the South,* Report ER 78-10008. Washington, D.C.: CIA, National Foreign Assessment Center, January 1978.

Cho, Soon-sung, Tae-hwan Kwak, John Chay, and Shannon McCune, Eds. *U.S.-Korean Relations, 1882–1982.* Seoul: Kyungnam University Press, 1982.

Clough, Ralph N. *Deterrence and Defense in Korea: The Role of U.S. Forces.* Washington, D.C.: The Brookings Institution, 1976.

Clough, Ralph N. *Embattled Korea.* Boulder: Westview Press, 1987.

Cumings, Bruce. *The Two Koreas.* Headline Series No. 269. New York: Foreign Policy Association, Inc., 1984.

Curtis, Gerald L. and Sung-joo Han, Eds. *The U.S.-South Korean Alliance; Evolving Patterns in Security Relations.* Lexington, MA: Lexington Books, 1983.

Han, Sung-joo. *The Failure of Democracy in South Korea.* Berkeley: University of California Press, 1974.

Han, Sung-joo, Ed. *After One Hundred Years: Continuity and Change in Korean-American Relations.* Seoul: Asiatic Research Center, Korea University, 1982.

Harrison, Selig S. *The South Korean Political Crisis and American Policy Options.* Washington: The Washington Institute Press, 1987.

Henderson, Gregory. *Korea: The Politics of the Vortex.* Cambridge: Harvard University Press, 1968.

Hinton, Harold C. *Korea Under New Leadership: The Fifth Republic.* New York; Praeger Publishers, 1983.

Human Rights in Korea. New York: Asia Watch Committee, 1985.

Hwang, In K. *The Neutralized Unification of Korea in Perspective.* Cambridge: Schenkman Publishing Co. Inc., 1980.

Kihl, Young Whan. *Politics and Policies in Divided Korea: Regimes in Contest.* Boulder, Colorado: Westview, 1984.

Kim, C.I. Eugene and B.C. Koh., Eds. *Journey to North Korea: Personal Perceptions.* Berkeley: Institute of East Asian Studies, University of California, 1983.

Koh, Byung Chul. *The Foreign Policy Systems of North and South Korea.* Berkeley: University of California Press, 1984.

Koo, Youngnok, and Sung-joo Han, Eds. *The Foreign Policy of the Republic of Korea.* New York: Columbia University Press, 1985.

Koo, Youngnok, and Dae-Sook Suh, eds. *Korea and the United States: A Century of Cooperation.* Honolulu: University of Hawaii Press, 1984.

Krauss, Melvyn. "It's Time for U.S. Troops to Leave Korea," *The Christian Science Monitor,* August 24, 1987, p. 13.

Korea; A Teacher's Guide. New York: The Asia Society, 1986.

Korea at the Crossroads: Implications for American Policy. New York: Council on Foreign Relations/The Asia Society, 1987.

Kwak, Tae-Hwan. *In Search of Peace and Unification on the Korean Peninsula.* Seoul: Seoul Computer Press, 1986.

Kwak, Tae-Hwan, Wayne Patterson, & Edward A. Olsen, Eds. *The Two Koreas in World Politics.* Seoul: Kyungnam University Press, 1983.

Lee, Ki-baik. *A New History of Korea.* Cambridge: Harvard University Press, 1984.

Matray, James I. *The Reluctant Crusade: American Foreign Policy in Korea, 1941–1950.* Honolulu: University of Hawaii Press, 1984.

McCormack, Gavan and Mark Selden, Eds. *Korea, North and South: The Deepening Crisis.* New York and London: Monthly Review Press, 1978.

Morse, Ronald A., Ed. *A Century of United States-Korean Relations: Proceedings of a Conference at the Wilson Center, June 17–19, 1982.* Washington, D.C.: University Press of America, Inc., 1983.

Moskowitz, Karl., Ed. *From Patron to Partner: The Development of U.S.-Korean Business and Trade Relations.* Lexington, MA: Lexington Books, 1984.

Nam, Joo-hong. *America's Commitment to South Korea; The First Decade of The Nixon Doctrine.* London: LSE Monographs in International Studies, 1986.

Oliver, Robert T. *Syngman Rhee and American Involvement in Korea, 1942–1960.* Seoul: Panmun Book Co., Ltd., 1973.

Polomka, Peter. "The Two Koreas: Catalyst for Conflict in East Asia?" *Adelphi Papers 208.* London: The International Institute for Strategic Studies, 1986.

Sandusky, Michael. *America's Parallel*. Alexandria, VA: Old Dominion Press, 1985.

Scalapino, Robert A. and Jun-yop Kim, Eds. *North Korea Today: Strategic and Domestic Issues*. Berkeley: Institute of East Asian Studies, University of California, 1983.

Scalapino, Robert A. *The U.S. and Korea: Looking Ahead*. Beverly Hills, CA: SAGE Publications, 1979.

Sullivan, John and Roberta Foss, Eds. *Two Koreas—One Future?* Lanham, MD: University Press of America/American Friends Service Committee, 1987.

Sunoo, Harold Hakwon. *America's Dilemma In Asia: The Case of South Korea*. Chicago: Nelson-Hall, 1979.

United States-Korean Trade Issues. Seoul: American Chamber of Commerce In Korea, June 1987.

White, Nathan. *U.S. Policy Toward Korea: Analyses, Alternatives and Recommendations*. Boulder: Westview Press, 1979.

Woronoff, Jon. *Korea's Economy: Man-Made Miracle*. Seoul: Sisa-yong-o-sa Publishers Inc., 1983.

SELECTED RELATED WORKS BY THE AUTHOR

US-Japan Strategic Reciprocity. Stanford: Hoover Institution Press, 1985.

"North Korea" in J.E. Katz, Ed. *Arms Production & Trade in Developing Countries*. Lexington, MA: Lexington Books, 1984.

"Japan and Korea" in W. Arnold & R. Ozaki, Eds. *Japan's Foreign Economic Relations in the 1980s*. Lexington, MA: Lexington Books, 1984.

"The Societal Role of the ROK Armed Forces" in E.A. Olsen & S. Jurika, Eds. *The Armed Forces in Contemporary Asian Societies*. Boulder: Westview Press, 1986.

"Republic of Korea" in R. Jones & S. Hildreth, Eds. *Emerging Powers: Defense & Security in the Third World.* New York: Praeger Publishers, 1986.

"The Sea of Japan" in Y.H. Kihl & L.E. Grinter, Eds. *Asian-Pacific Security: Emerging Challenges and Responses.* New York: St. Martin's Press, 1987.

" 'Korea, Inc.': The Political Impact of Park Chung-hee's Economic Miracle," *ORBIS,* Spring 1980.

"The United States' Korea Policy: Offering Pyongyang An Economic Carrot," *The Journal of Northeast Asian Studies,* Fall 1982.

"Nichi-bei-kan sogo anpo taisei o nozomu" (Desiring a Japan-US-ROK Mutual Defense System), *Chuo Koron,* February 1983.

"The Evolution of the ROK's Foreign Policy," *Washington Quarterly,* Winter 1983.

"Security in Northeast Asia: A Trilateral Alternative," *Naval War College Review,* January-February 1985.

" 'Chiipu raida' e no fuman" (Criticism of a "Cheap Rider"), *Chuo Koron,* December, 1985.

"The Arms Race on The Korean Peninsula," *Asian Survey,* August 1986.

"Korean Political Uncertainty and U.S. Policy," *Washington Quarterly,* Spring 1987.

"Keeping North Korea Out of Soviet Hands," *Far Eastern Economic Review,* May 15, 1987.

"Korean Politics and U.S. Policy: Higher Pressure and Lower Profile," *Asian Survey,* August 1987.

"The Maritime Strategy in the Western Pacific," *Naval War College Review,* Autumn 1987.

"A Case for Strategic Protectionism," *Strategic Review,* Fall 1987.